CATHOLIC THOUGHT IN CRISIS

CATHOLIC THOUGHT IN CRISIS is one of the volumes in a new series, IMPACT BOOKS, designed to bring to the modern reader the significant achievements of scholars, both Catholic and non-Catholic, in the fields of Scripture, Theology, Philosophy, Mathematics, History, and the Physical and Social Sciences. IMPACT BOOKS will explore these realms of human knowledge in order to give the average man some idea of the work being carried on today within them and in order to lay a basis for fruitful dialogue between men of different interests and persuasions on questions vital to all mankind.

Catholic Thought
in Crisis

REV. PETER RIGA

ST. JOHN VIANNEY SEMINARY
EAST AURORA, NEW YORK

THE BRUCE PUBLISHING COMPANY

MILWAUKEE

NIHIL OBSTAT:

STEPHANUS GERENCSER, S.T.D.
Censor Deputatus
die 5 Junii, 1962

IMPRIMATUR:

✠JOSEPHUS ALOISIUS BURKE
Episcopus Buffalensis
die 7 Junii, 1962

BX 1751.2
R56

Library of Congress Catalog Card Number: 63–14921

FOR A DEAR FRIEND

"O altitudo divitiarum sapientiae et scientiae Dei"

(Rom 11:33)

INTRODUCTION

THE modern world continues to change at such a pace that the Catholic of our era finds it increasingly difficult to grapple with its problems. It is difficult to adjust to change and painful to acquire new habits of thought. If this has been the constant experience of the Church for 2000 years, what can compare with the awesome revolutions in twentieth-century society? Social, international, economic, scientific, and even philosophic trends have been so revolutionary in the past 100 years that the problems they pose to the modern Catholic might well be called staggering. If anyone thinks this statement exaggerated he has only to investigate each of these fields for himself. Even a superficial glance into their modern evolution will show the truth of this statement. We have entered the era of interplanetary space conquests; economic interdependency of all nations is already achieved; nuclear and thermonuclear energy promises an unprecedented era of either total annihilation of the human race or of progress unknown in the history of man; the brotherhood of man and the need for international justice are recognized by all nations, locked as they are in a deadly conflict between Communism and the democracies of the West. These are but a few of the gigantic problems which the Christian must face up to if he is to be faithful to the command of Christ: "teach all nations." The ugly fact of the matter, moreover, is that, in general, Catholics have not really faced the modern world and its problems.

How shall this Christian message be made known to the people of the revolutionary twentieth century? To say that Christ and, with Him, the Christian are not interested in what is happening in this modern "world" is surely to relegate Christianity to a pietistic private affair of no consequence to modern man. Such a view, moreover, is far from St. Paul's vision of cosmic redemption. Modern theologians have done great service to Catholic thought by grappling with these momentous problems and by attempting a real, although somewhat incomplete, theological synthesis of the technological and scientific phases of our era. The central factor in their synthesis is the position which the layman must play in the total consecration of modern society and its orientations to Christ. In general, this is what they have had to say with regard to this whole movement. The layman has his proper function in the Church. Consequently, his proper spirituality and sanctification must be sought in fulfilling that specific work which is his. In other words, his proper function is the incarnation of the divine life into the temporal domain, and in fulfilling this work he will reach his own spiritual goal. With the eyes of faith (for faith is nothing more than God's vision of all reality, celestial and terrestrial, engrafted onto ours) he must enter fully and unreservedly into the temporal in all of its ramifications to bring out the image of God contained in it. He is, in the true biblical sense of the word, God's lieutenant in creation, prolonging creation according to the image of God and man given to him in faith. His proper mortification, if you will, will be to purify continuously his own intentions and not to be perturbed that, at times, he sees no direct connection between his work and the kingdom, the supernatural as such. If faith is demanded in God's mysteries — for we can never understand them fully — so too is faith required for the restoring of the temporal order to God, for we do not fully understand all its ramifications and consequences. But one thing must remain certain: in his research, his laboratory, at his machine, at his microscope, in his struggle for just laws and social justice, on his tractor on an American farm or in an underdeveloped country, the layman is doing God's will in prolonging creation and fulfilling his proper apostolate in the Church of God. In this sense, the layman partakes of the work of the Church in its full and cosmic sense. It was St. Paul himself who had this gigantic and total vision of the Church and Christ's triumph through it:

> He is the image of the invisible God, the first-born of every creature, because in him were created all creatures in the heavens and on the earth, both visible and invisible, whether Thrones, or Dominations, or Principalities, or Powers. All have been created through him and for him. He exists prior to all creatures, and in him they are all preserved in being. Further, he is the head of his body, the Church. . . . For it pleased God the Father that in him all fullness should dwell, and that through him God should reconcile to himself every being and make peace both on earth and in heaven through the blood shed on the cross.[1]

The lay Christian has a tremendous dignity, for he is to subdue all things to Christ. But to do this, the Christian must see all things as Christ sees them and work to bring out His image in them, whether those things are technology, science, psychology, law, sociology, art, or culture. His proper vocation as a layman is to bring out Christ's image, to find it within things and consecrate himself to it. In virtue of creation all is Christ's *by right;* the great dignity of the lay Christian will be to help make it His, *in fact,* enabling Christ to reproduce His image, prolonging it in creation. To change socioeconomic structures so many can live as men and not as slaves to the earth is a direct work of Christ; to humanize laws of punishment and labor is a direct work of Christ; to guarantee a climate of freedom and tolerance, respect of property and human beings under and by just laws, is a direct work of Christ; to aid underdeveloped countries attain the material capacity to live in the freedom of human beings is a work of Christ; to work for peace in the UN and other international organizations is a direct work of Christ; to devote one's life to research for better health, that men may live their lives comparatively free from mortal dangers, is a direct work of Christ; to dedicate one's life to bringing out the image and

---

[1] Col 1:15–20.

aspirations of man in art and writing is a direct work of Christ; to fight racial discrimination by legislation and personal example is a direct work of Christ; to work for equitable international trade agreements and tariffs is a direct work of Christ — and so forth throughout the whole gamut of the body temporal. A grandiose tableau indeed presents itself to the Catholic layman. And strange as it may seem, only he can do this work. Communism and other totalitarian ideologies can only lead man to self-destruction, because they view the temporal wrongly. Only the Catholic layman has at his disposal the spiritual and Christlike vision which will lead the temporal to the glorification of God and service to his fellowman. The layman's is an awesome responsibility, but one which can be shirked only at the terrible price of losing the modern world and modern man to Christ. Every other religion is radically incapable of such a theological endeavor because of some basic incompatibility with its own internal structure: the Eastern religions because they deny either matter itself or its positive value; materialism, Communism, and secularism because they reject the realm of spirit. Must, then, the men of our day despair? The responsibility of this grave theological question depends on an *integral* Christian theological synthesis which is and can be its only authentic answer. Our age longs for a "substantial soul," an inner meaning to its human values and accomplishments. There is a constant temptation to condemn or make little of human and temporal realities. All the dualist doctrines which consider matter the work of an evil principle and fundamentally bad have yielded to this temptation. The material universe is, nevertheless, willed by God. And this world that we see and touch is re-created by the Incarnation. By reason of his nature, man stands on the horizon between matter and spirit; he is the bond of friendship uniting and glorifying all creation, according to the beautiful expression of St. Hilary, and capable of giving a meaning to the material universe.

Only future historians will be able to say whether we have helped solve the problem or negated it by ignoring it in any form of escape. In that proportion will future Catholic historians either condemn or commend us. Our responsibility is terrible, but the challenge is too great to be avoided.

In the following pages, we hope to show how theologians of our day have integrated these aspects into various directions or orientations. We have divided the work into three parts, each of which has a tremendous significance for the lay Christian of our day. The first two sections — namely Christian humanism and the theological concept of the lay Christian — have to do with the definition of the layman and his proper orientation to the modern technical world. The third section (religious freedom) has to do with what probably is the greatest single problem affecting the relationship between Catholicism and both Christian and non-Christian sects. The attitude which the Christian takes to this problem will spell either success or failure for any future apostolate of the Catholic to the world.

There is every reason to be optimistic. At the opening of the Second Vatican Council, as *Time* reported, "the bouncy old man of 82 who is Pope John XXIII told the assembled bishops that this is no time for pessimism; there is too much work to be done."

East Aurora, N. Y.
Feast of the Conversion of St. Paul, 1962

CONTENTS

PART I

THE CHRISTIAN AND THE TEMPORAL ORDER

INTRODUCTION

DURING the past few years, Catholic theologians have turned their attention more seriously to the Christian evaluation of the temporal order.[1] The terms used to express this direction in recent theology are many: theology of terrestrial realities, Christian humanism, the Christian participation in the temporal order, consecration of the world, etc. Whatever the terms used, the essential preoccupation of theologians has been to examine the diverse values of the temporal order with a view to determine their Christian signification. What do progress, technology, work, the material universe, the body, and so forth mean for the Christian? In a highly technological civilization such as ours this question has become paramount. Nor can we restrict this notion of "technological civilization" to the West; recent developments in underdeveloped countries, pushed on by both the Western and Communist blocs, have brought even the most backward nations to a realization that technology and the development of their proper resources hold the answer and hope for the future. Africa, the Near and Far East are all feverishly in the process of technological change and advancement. What, it is asked, can Catholic theology contribute to all this? Shall we leave the philosophical interpretation and direction of these changes to atheistic Marxism? Is there nothing more in this "technological revolution" of the past 100 years than a struggle among the various strata of society or a movement toward economic betterment? And what of the sciences themselves? Can we see any development in them other than the bringing to the surface of the potentialities already put there

---

[1] Cf. works cited in the Bibliographical Note to this Part, pp. 44–55.

2

by the Creator? In what way do the technician, doctor, psychologist, social worker further Christ's kingdom on earth? What Christian signification and orientation can we give these diverse developments in the temporal order?

This question has occupied the thought of the Holy Fathers themselves through these past 50 years. Faced with the attempt of modern ideologies to use scientific and technological progress against religion, the Popes have attempted to show the harmony between the profane activities of men and their supernatural vocation. A book has recently been consecrated to pontifical documents of the past 50 years with reference to the human body and its Christian signification.[2] More recently, His Holiness John XXIII has given the world a masterpiece of social doctrine: *Mater et Magistra*. In it, the Holy Father shows deep concern over the underdeveloped nations of the world and voices the hope that technology and Christian charity will alleviate their misery.

The necessities and revolutionary character of modern times must certainly explain this new theological orientation. It is not an exaggeration to say that the challenges the Church has faced in the past 100 years must explain the rethinking of the position of the layman in the Church. The age when the notion of "perfection" was relegated to the religious life or to the monastery has long since passed. Today we speak more and more of the position of the layman in the Church, his proper mission of bringing Christ into the world by consecrating the world by and through the ideals of Christ. In other words, the trend today in the development of a theology of the layman is to define him in function of the temporal which is his proper domain. Laymen are immersed in the temporal and are to work out their salvation in, and not in spite of, their temporal tasks. Theologians commonly teach that one's duty of state is

---

[2] *The Human Body* (Boston, 1960). See also, in this same Papal Text series, *The Lay Apostolate* (1959) and *The Woman in the Modern World* (1960). The publishers have announced a new title, *Peace Within the Nation and International Peace*. All of these studies are preoccupied with a concern to show the Christian's role in the modern world.

the primary means of arriving at sanctification. Therefore, for the layman, interest in temporal affairs is not only necessary and praiseworthy, it is vital. It is only in and by the temporal that laymen will sanctify themselves. What, then, can Catholic theology tell them of the meaning of their professional work, their business, their medicine, their industry? Can theology give this work of the layman in the world a true human signification, or must it be treated as a sort of "basket-weaving," a meaningless exercise whereby the layman fills up the timespace between birth and death?[3] It is incumbent on the Catholic theologian to give Catholic laymen a religious and Christian sense of their "profane" activities such as medicine, economics, psychology, sociology, politics, work, and, in short, all human activity in and on the world as distinguished from the "sacred." In the words of Pope John XXIII:

> From what we have briefly touched upon above, let none of our sons conclude, and especially the laity, that they act prudently if, in regard to the transitory affairs of this life, they become quite remiss in their specific Christian contributions. On the contrary, we reaffirm that they should be daily more zealous in carrying out this role.
>
> Indeed, when Christ Our Lord made that solemn prayer for the unity of His Church, He asked this from the Father on behalf of His disciples: "I do not pray that thou take them out of the world, but that thou keep them from evil" (Jn 17:15). Let no one imagine that there is any opposition between these two things so that they cannot be properly reconciled: namely, the perfection of one's own soul and the business of this life, as if one had no choice but to abandon the activities of this world in order to strive for Christian perfection, or as if one could not attend to these pursuits without endangering his own dignity as a man and as a Christian.
>
> However, it is in full accord with the designs of God's providence that men develop and perfect themselves by exercise of their daily tasks, for this is the lot of practically everyone in the affairs of this mortal life (*Mater et Magistra*, par. 254–255).

---

[3] On this point, see John C. Murray, S.J., "Is It Basket-Weaving?" in *We Hold These Truths* (New York, 1960), pp. 175–196.

These words of the Holy Father could not be more perfect to describe our present intentions in writing these pages.

These questions on the Christian signification of the temporal are, therefore, of vital concern and interest to the Catholic world of today. Theologians, moreover, have not neglected to explore the relations between the temporal and eternal, the "sacred" and the "profane," the "incarnational" and the "eschatological," the natural and the supernatural. For well over a decade various attempts have been made to harmonize their relationships through the development of a theology of work, progress, culture, history, and technology. Our purpose is to sketch in outline form the various orientations and solutions which Catholic theologians have given to these trends. Our study will attempt to set forth some biblical and theological considerations essential, to our mind, for reaching a Christian interpretation of terrestrial realities, following this with an explanation of the two more prominent attempts to give this interpretation and of the subsequent efforts of theologians to tackle such specific questions as the theology of work, the theology of history, the theology of science, etc. In reality, these efforts represent the initial response of the Church to the challenge of the modern world.

CHAPTER I

THE MEANING OF TERRESTRIAL REALITIES

Some Biblical Considerations

THERE is little doubt that the Bible itself on numerous occasions gives us a rather striking anthropology, or, in more simple terms, the meaning of man and his reality in the eyes of God, *sub oculo Dei*. In other words, creation and man have, for God, a definite religious meaning in the Old Testament: Creation, including man, is God's work;[1] men belong to Him and He does with them as He wills;[2] all serve His purposes and His designs,[3] even those who do not know Him and who sin.[4] The nations themselves are the instruments of God.[5] He need but whistle, as a man would whistle for his dog, and the Assyrians do His work.[6] God is mingled in human affairs — and unless they are built and done under His direction and will, they are as nothing.[7] With the New Testament, we see a fuller picture of human values considered from the point of view of God's intentions: the Word became flesh[8] and after His death took His human flesh into heaven with Him where it is not to be sepa-

---

[1] Gn 1:27. See W. Eichrodt, *Theology of the Old Testament* (Philadelphia, 1961), pp. 289–319.
[2] Ps 135 (134):10 ff.
[3] Is 10:1–14.
[4] Is 46:8–12.
[5] Is 8:7
[6] Is 5:26; Za 10:8.
[7] Ps 126:1–8.
[8] Jn 1:7.

6

rated from His person again.[9] Pain, sickness, and death have been given a redemptive role in the Christian context;[10] marriage, the most fundamental of human institutions, is raised to the dignity of a sacrament;[11] indeed, creation waits for the redemption of man and in the meantime is in pain of growth and travail.[12] Peace, joy, concord, and justice are the fruits of the Spirit and the expected qualities in each Christian life;[13] they cannot remain individual or personal, but must go out first to the Mystical Body of Christ[14] and then to all men if possible.[15] All human reality falls under the dichotomy of "flesh-spirit" (sarx-pneuma) in the Pauline sense of these words; this means that all men can and must serve Christ or be opposed to Him. The epistle to the Ephesians is clearly about a redemption which goes beyond the salvation of individuals;[16] it is truly a Christian anthropology and cosmology of the whole of creation, inclusive of the world of men and their values.

Thus, in capsule form, we see that God, the Lord of history, has given a value to the realities of this world and to man, conferring on them a vital role in the economy of creation and redemption. In other words, there is such a thing as a revealed anthropology in the Bible, and we would do well to study its fundamental traits.

We have mentioned the Pauline notion of the dichotomy between "flesh" and "spirit," sarx and pneuma. Paul's statement is most interesting with regard to any theology of the temporal. The meaning of these two words is paramount here.

For St. Paul the word pneuma (spirit) means primarily God Himself as communicated to men. The word is also used in reference to man insofar as he uses all his faculties according to the designs and wishes of God. It signifies, more particularly, the intelligence of man illuminated by the gift of God, by His divine grace. "Pneumatic" (spiritual), then, means that all of

---

[9] Nicene Creed: "and of His kingdom there will be no end."
[10] Rom 6:5–8.
[11] Eph 5:22–33.
[12] Rom 8:18–23.
[13] Gal 5:22.
[14] Col 2:17–20.
[15] Rom 12:17–18.
[16] Eph 5:19; cf. Col 1:9; 1 Cor 2:15.

man's faculties (inclusive of his mind, body, desires, tendencies) are used according to God's plan and wish. It does not necessarily mean the intellectual as opposed to the physical, the immaterial as opposed to the material. On the contrary, a proud man may be very "intellectual" philosophically but he is by no means spiritual ("pneumatic"), since his intelligence is not directed by the Holy Spirit but by his egoism and pride. Even the body and its desires are "spiritual" when, for example, the Christian abstains from fornication since his body is the temple of the Holy Spirit.[17]

By "flesh" Paul, and other New Testament writers as well, designates those who are led not by the Spirit but by their own light of reason, by their own desires and wishes as opposed to those of God. "Fleshy" is all that resists the kingdom of the spirit. It does not mean nor is it in any way the equivalent of flesh in the sense of physical reality. As a matter of fact, in the epistle to the Galatians, St. Paul makes a summary list of the works of the flesh.[18] Among these are found some things that are in no way "flesh" in the physical sense, v.g., envy, hate, disputes, dissensions, etc.

This distinction of St. Paul must not be confused with the Greek conceptions of "body-soul" and the dichotomy between the realities signified by these concepts. As a matter of fact, Semitic thought knew of no such dichotomy. Paul's analysis is not that of the Greek philosophers of matter (body) and of the spiritual principle (soul), nor could it be. A fortiori, neither St. Paul nor any of the writers of the New Testament ever conceived of a gnostic dualism where the soul is imprisoned in a quasi-evil principle, the body. For the writers of the New Testament, the body was simply an integral part of man, who was created as one whole by God, destined entirely either for death or for life. This point is central, for it radically distinguishes the thought of the Bible from Greek philosophy. It is

---

[17] 1 Cor 2:10–16. For a penetrating study of St. Paul's understanding of "flesh-spirit," see J. A. Robinson, *The Body: A Study in Pauline Theology* (London, 1957).
[18] Gal 5:19–21.

central, too, because it shows that matter as such is God's creation and, consequently, good. This contrasts, perhaps, with a segment of Catholic thought which has been influenced too greatly by Greek philosophy and not nourished enough from the sources of revelation.[19] Unconsciously at least, Greek influence led to a depreciation of human and temporal values in Christian life. And this depreciation has been the source of a certain impoverishment of the sense of the religious in temporal matters and affairs.

The meaning St. Paul expressed through the "flesh-spirit" dichotomy is conveyed in various other ways in Scripture: light and darkness, love and hate, life and death, truth and falsehood all have the same sense. All of these expressions have in common a double aspect: metaphysical and universal.

They are *metaphysical* insofar as light and darkness, for example, are not simply predicated of the mind, but of all reality. The light is the manifestation of the divine attributes in the world and in man; darkness is all of reality insofar as it is in opposition to God. Here the meaning is the same as we have seen with the antithesis flesh-spirit. It is here that we have the theological definition of the real, of all reality from a biblical point of view.

These terms are also *universal* in their signification, for they comprehend all reality, both created and uncreated. There can be absolutely nothing which lies beyond the categories designated by these terms. All reality is good or bad insofar as it conforms or does not conform to these criteria. These biblical notions contain religious as well as profane activities and orientations. All things must be measured in accordance with this biblical norm and from it will draw their Christian signification. The repercussions of these notions in the profane activities of

---

[19] This can be exaggerated. Christianity owes at least some debt of gratitude to Greek thought in and through its technical formulation and explanation of Catholic doctrine. Many non-Catholics have exaggerated in accusing Catholics of sacrificing biblical thought for Greek thought; cf. A. Nygren, *Eros and Agape* (London, 1955) and the Catholic answer by Martin C. D'Arcy, *The Mind and Heart of Love* (London, 1956).

men are more than evident. All of creation is called upon to
come back to its originating principle who is Christ: "All things
came into being through him, and without him there came to
be not one thing that has come to be."[20] St. Paul expresses the
same idea by an accusative of intention: "All things were made
through and *unto* him."[21] Pertinent here is O. Cullmann's
wise observation that "the Church and the world cannot be
represented by two juxtaposed circles . . . they are not like
two circles which coincide either. On the contrary, we must
represent them as two concentric circles whose center is formed
by Christ. The *total* surface is the *regnum Christi*."[22]

It will be up to the *membrum Christi*, in whom is manifest
the living Christ, to bring this value to the world. Since the
biblical analysis is all-inclusive and cosmic in origin and intention, the Christian must endeavor to bring about the renewal
of all things in Christ in all of his tasks, be they "sacred" in
the proper sense or profane. Both categories of the sacred-
profane are, therefore, within the confines of the religious, since
the operations of flesh-spirit, light-darkness, etc., are both metaphysical and universal. Creation and redemption in and by and
for Christ is certainly *de jure*, but it has not as yet come about
de facto. The Christian himself must bring about this kingdom
of Christ in his total activity, both sacred and profane. The gift
of the spirit given to him in baptism calls for a *total* transformation and transposition of all his activities, desires, thoughts.
For just as the Christian has been totally transformed by this
gift of the spirit and just as the Christian is another living
cell in Christ, so too must he transpose this living cell to the
totality of his activities and orientations, be they psychological,
social, cultural, or religious. He must be the living cell at the
beginning of the new creation which "groans and travails in
pain until now, waiting for the adoption as sons, the redemp-

20 Jn 1:3.
21 Col 1:16 (Conf. tr.).
22 *Christ and Time* (London, 1952), p. 188; Y. Congar, *Lay People in the
Church* (London, 1957), pp. 73–102.

tion of our body."[23] This passage has a tremendous impact on the Christian who sees in it all the exhaustiveness of the soteriology of St. Paul. Most Christians do not see, as St. Paul did so clearly, this insertion of man and his redemption in the totality of creation. Christians habitually picture Christ in His relationship to individual Christians as savior of their souls. Yet this view does violence to the thought of St. Paul. The Apostle of the Gentiles saw the repercussions of creation and redemption not only on the individual Christian but on the whole cosmos, the whole universe. The salvific work of Christ extends itself to all of creation and has marked everything with the sign of the cross.

The biblical interpretation of man's activity is therefore very rich in possibilities. Specific applications, of course, are nowhere to be found in the scriptural texts. These will have to be worked out within the confines of a sane theology. According to the Bible, then, all creation is good; it belongs to Christ in a very special way, since He created and redeemed it. The Christian is inserted into Christ as a new living cell, and inserted as well into the totality of Christ's redemptive work with regard to the whole cosmos. In furthering Christ as a *membrum Christi,* his activities will have definite meaning in bringing about the redemption not only of individual Christians but also of all creation, in which he finds himself an integral part. Creation must share in the redemption by and through the Christian. In this context, the "profane" activities of Christians have a real and concrete signification, a profoundly religious meaning.

Theological Elaboration

It would be a painful as well as an unjustifiable limitation of this study to consider only what the Bible has to say concerning the significance of the temporal order. The Bible has certain orientations to aid us in our research but it, too, is limited in its scope and in its penetration into our problem.

---

[23] Rom 8:22–23. See corresponding text of Gn 3:15 with regard to the subjection of all creation to man's sin.

We must appeal to theology as such, which uses for the premises of its conclusions both revealed truth and natural reason. This is not to betray the Word of God, as Karl Barth would have us believe,[24] but to use the totality of God's creation in the service of truth. The Protestant conception along these lines will be fundamentally pessimistic and negative, for it sees man as having been fundamentally corrupted by sin — he can, consequently, no longer trust his reason but only God's Word, which alone is true.[25] The argument against this view could be put in this light: the whole world is called to become similar to God. Yet God is actually goodness, harmony, and perfection itself. He wills, moreover, to communicate Himself to us, to "dwell" in us, to make us "Godlike" — reflections of His harmony, order, goodness, and holiness. God, then, has formed man according to His own likeness.[26] This is certainly one of the great teachings of the book of Genesis. This divine exemplarism will permit us to understand more fully the theological meaning inherent in all of creation *insofar as it reflects the image of the Creator.* This is in no way a sort of symbolism: it is, in a very true way, the theological definition of things. This divine exemplarism needs to be more fully developed, and its fruits will be repaid in a more Christian understanding of the temporal order.

Most people realize very little that one of the first Christian victories over heresy was a defense of the visibility and the value of the temporal against the charges of gnostic writers. The gnostics, who were the first Christian heretics, held that material creation was, at most, evil, and that it was destined for destruction. The answer to this heresy was clear and unequivocal: all of creation is good because it was created and

---

[24] Karl Barth, *The Word of God and the Word of Man* (New York, 1957), p. 55.

[25] *Ibid.*, p. 58. This statement, however, needs some clarification, as this notion seems to be undergoing somewhat of a change in contemporary Protestant circles. Contemporary Protestantism does not universally retain the "vitiated nature" concept of Luther. On this, see the last chapter of Murray's *We Hold These Truths* (New York, 1960), pp. 295–336.

[26] Gn 1:27; Col 2:17.

ordained by God: "maker of all things, visible and invisible."
The sense of these early doctors was clear: they wanted to save
the world of matter from the disdain of the gnostics and the
condemnations of the Neoplatonists. The body of the Word-
made-flesh was real, just as was the bread of the Eucharist and
the water of baptism; all this had a sense for eternity and a
divine signification; the earth was holy in its origin as a work
of God. But that was only half of the theological task which
faced these early theologians and which has come down to us
today: when we have defined the act of creation as divine, there
still remains the tremendous task of discovering what new sense
can be derived from these created objects, the deeper potentialities with which the creator has invested them. Thus, theology has before it an enormous task. Before we can tell men
how they must act with created things, we must first show them
the divine vision of creation; the divine sense of the world and
of life, of work and the land, of health and suffering, of industrial progress and sports, of travel and the home, of the body
and the soul, of tears and love, of human labor and sweat. And
only a sane dogmatic theology can show this divine sense of
created things. "We must have a great faith to arrive at the
harmonious union of the work of God's hands; for all that is,
was created by You, my God, and we must love all of Your
work as You love it, with a love without reserve."[27]

This requires a continuous activity of man on creation. From
the first pages of Genesis we see that man is called, in a sense,
to collaborate with God in the work of creation. Man is God's
lieutenant who is to dominate "the fish of the sea, the birds
of the air, the animals and all the earth" precisely because man
is created in the "image and likeness of God." Man's image
and likeness to God is precisely that, like God, man has a share
in the domination of the earth. And in a very true sense, man
will continue creation by his further activity over what has been
initially given to him by God. Thus, creation is good in a double

---

[27] M. Legant, La Condition Chrétienne (Paris, 1946), p. 24; J. Mouroux,
The Meaning of Man (New York, 1948), pp. 1–18.

sense: good in its divine origin and good also in all the potentialities which are derived from this initial creation by the
further "creation" of man. The virtualities written in things by
divine wisdom are good in their principle, and their development can only be a gain for the universe and for man. As a
matter of fact, in developing these potentialities, man brings
out in himself the "image of God" with which he was invested at the beginning of creation. By furthering God's work,
he achieves the divine image in himself as co-creator with the
living God. Man's vocation as the image of his Creator is
intimately bound up with his task in the world.

In conclusion we can sum up the theological argument as
follows: human realities, of whatever order they be, can have
a religious, even though not a sacred, meaning. Every creature,
and by creature we also mean man's creation of art, society,
technology, science, music, sculpture, trade, etc., is in its root
good. We have seen that for the Christian and the Bible, all
creation is good.

These notions, then, of the image of God in man and the
kingship of Christ through creation and redemption seem to
offer Catholic theologians the greatest possibilities of a spiritual
and religious interpretation of temporal values.

The notion of kingship of Christ to be spread abroad by
Christians seems to be pregnant with meaning in this regard.
The recent popes have insisted on the fact that the kingship of
Christ is not to be relegated to the purely "religious" — once
again a sort of Josephism of the twentieth century — as has
been too often the painful case since the Middle Ages. This
kingship and domination is His by creation and by redemption,
and the problem has been to distinguish the two levels of
existence (natural — supernatural) and at the same time to give
them each their *religious* signification for Christ and the kingdom. The problem has been acute for over 200 years, but it
is especially so in our own day. We are in the midst of a vast
sociological, technological, and scientific revolution. The day
is forever gone when the secular or the temporal was integrated,

or rather, we should say, subordinated, to the spiritual properly speaking. Today we have arrived at the opposite swing of the pendulum when secularism has become the dominant element in society and when the temporal, as manifested in technological and scientific humanism, has been neutral if not actually inimical to the Christian message. Let us attempt to see some solutions to this dilemma.

CHAPTER II

ESCHATOLOGICAL OR INCARNATIONAL?

Some Catholic Solutions

THE challenge offered by modern technology and scientific progress to Catholic theology for integrating specific values of the temporal order within the perspective of the Gospel has not gone unanswered. Such theologians as Congar, Thils, Dubarle, Maritain, Mouroux, and Ong have tried to give some sort of a theological interpretation to this problem, which preoccupies man today more than ever before.[1] Can the temporal as such have a theological interpretation? To this question there has been a whole variety of answers, but they can be reduced to two: the eschatological, which by and large urges the faithful to neglect mundane affairs in order to give wholehearted attention to the invisible things of the Spirit; and the incarnational, which sees a genuine Christian value in terrestrial realities. The two viewpoints are inclusive of the temporal order in all its ramifications. Throughout the Christian era there have been many attempts, such as those of Bossuet and St. Augustine, to integrate the temporal sphere into the religious as far as human history is concerned. But in general we would have to conclude with Pierre Teilhard de Chardin: "I do not think I am exaggerating when I say that nine out of ten practicing Christians feel that man's work is always at the level of a

---

[1] For the writings of these thinkers on this question, see the Bibliographical Note to Part I, pp. 44–55.

'spiritual encumbrance.' In spite of the practice of right intentions, and the day offered every morning to God, the general
run of the faithful dimly feel that time spent at the office or
studio, in the fields or in the factory, is time diverted from
prayer and adoration."[2]

But can we really say that created things and the temporal
order mean anything for Christ? Can we give a Christian meaning to these human endeavors and conquests themselves? It is
here that we are confronted with the two divergent attitudes
within the Catholic community mentioned above: one, the
so-called eschatological solution, which found support in Tertullian during the early days of the Church, is today represented
by such able defenders as Danielou and Bouyer; the other, the
incarnational, is held, for instance, by such men as Thils, Congar, and De Chardin, and its intellectual forebears include such
figures as Origen and St. Thomas Aquinas. What do these
diverse systems of thought hold with regard to the temporal?

The eschatological interpretation emphasizes the triviality of
earthly concerns in comparison to heavenly things. They are
merely shadows of the perfect things to come and are to be
discarded when the kingdom shall have arrived in its fullness.
This rather negative attitude is generated by the conviction that
this present world is destined for destruction, that it waits at
every turn to seduce man in his fallen nature, and that we are
to be distrustful of it. Because of God's utter transcendence,
nothing really counts except eternal life and what nourishes it.
This tendency emphasizes the virtue of renunciation and holds
that we are to escape the world's ways by contemplation of
the heavenly realities; if the Christian does his earthly work,
it is only because of his complete obedience to the will of God
and because he must suffer and prove his love of God by entering the world and its worries. This attitude undoubtedly has
much truth in it. Yet it is not a question here of denying the

---

[2] Pierre Teilhard de Chardin, *The Divine Milieu* (New York, 1960), p. 34.
This whole essay is most interesting for those who wish to study the relationship
between the temporal and Christ's kingdom.

truth contained in this view, but of measuring its correspondence to the total truth of the Gospels.

The incarnational interpretation, on the other hand, emphasizes the fact that God became man, and that somehow all matter has become sanctified by that fact. It cannot entirely be destined for total destruction, for it is good both in creation and redemption. In creation, God commanded man to continue His own work by "dominating" the earth and all therein, by being God's lieutenant. In a very true sense, then, man continues the work of creation by his work and his endeavor. "Work," claim the champions of this view, "is a goal in itself apart from any religious value we give it by making a morning offering."[3] In the words of Pius XI and Pius XII, the layman must "consecrate the world." Renouncement is certainly necessary in this scheme of things, but it is more a renouncement of egoism, a refusal to use one's talents or gifts for personal profit or gain, a rejection of the laziness and inertia which are the base products of our fallen nature. It is a renouncement of smugness and complacency, because it is Christ's reflection that we search for and discover in our unceasing labor. In this way there can be no incompatibility between following a purely secular vocation and our love of God. The two are not juxtaposed but intimately joined. With the eye of faith, all progress, all discovery leads to fresh insight of God and love of neighbor in harnessing means of the material for his comfort, for his healing, for his good as directed to the final end which is God. Nor will God utterly destroy what He has created. These theologians give as examples the ascended Body of Christ and His Mother, the matter of the sacraments, etc. They will be changed but never destroyed. "The more I examine myself, the more I discover this psychological truth: that no one lifts his little finger to do the smallest task unless moved, however obscurely, by the conviction that he is contributing infinitesimally . . . to your work, my God."[4]

---

[3] D. J. Geaney, "Some Notes on Lay Spirituality," *Worship*, 26 (1952), p. 115.   [4] De Chardin, *op. cit.*, p. 24.

We thus have the two tendencies in Christian thought relative to the meaning of the temporal. Both have elements of Christian truth. Both claim to have firm scriptural foundations. However, the eschatological view, by emphasizing sin as a permanent human fact casting a shadow over all human accomplishments and by stressing the utterly supernatural character of God's kingdom of grace, seems in the eyes of many Christian thinkers concerned with this question to lose sight of equally important aspects of the Gospel. Keenly appreciative of the truth that grace perfects nature and does not destroy it, these authors claim that the incarnational theory is in closer conformity to Christian tradition than is the eschatological. According to these authors, the eschatological theory is rather pessimistic and negative — a sort of "basket-weaving" with regard to God's creation. Incarnationalism, they hold, conforms to Scripture in the sense that it upholds men's collaboration with God in work which is good. It has the further advantage of giving a meaning to the role of the layman in the Church. If terrestrial realities have no meaning in themselves, then laymen are only wasting their time. But certainly it matters to Christ if there be equitable international trade agreements, peace among the nations of the world, just distribution and use of the world's goods for the good of all, equal treatment of rich and poor, white and colored, under just laws. Surely it matters to Him that religious values be reflected (as God's image in all creation) in art and literature, music and culture, on TV and films; surely He cares if children are protected from unscrupulous men of profit, that woman attain the dignity and vocation He has destined for her, that technology and science reflect the great beauties of nature which are His reflection and that they are used for the profit and good of all men for whom they were created; surely He cares, and cares deeply, that the sick be healed, the mentally ill aided, the lame walk, and the blind see. To say that there is no dignity — a religious and sacred dignity — in all these "profane" works is, according to these authors, tantamount to blasphemy. In and by his work, the layman will find God, whom he will see in the love of neighbor for whom he labors. To interpret all these works simply as ways of "making a living" is to add insult to injury. Certainly, because of our fallen natures, there is danger of using the products of our hands for personal glory, egoism, and selfishness, of making an idol of this reflection of God. Yet all this does not take away from the dignity of human work and endeavor — if only we have the "simple eye" of evangelical faith with which to see. The layman has, then, a grave obligation to involve himself in these tasks to a greater extent than does his pagan neighbor. The pagan can see no further than the gain, the work; for the Christian, material things are the reflection of God, the glory of his hands as God's son, and the aid and mutual assistance of his neighbor in love, even when there is nothing specifically religious or sacred in his labor.

Both of these attitudes are substantiated, to a degree, by certain biblical texts. This is only natural since the Bible does not pretend to give us a complete or integral anthropology; it is the duty of theology to elaborate the latter. Many, however, agree with Fr. Thils in saying that the Bible, in general, is much more optimistic in this regard than the pessimists (Eschatologists) would have us believe,[5] and that some form of evidence for a Christian meaning of the created and the temporal can be discerned in the Sacred Text. Granted that it does not give us the full picture and cannot accomplish its end by its own powers, these authors still believe that, from the texts, there is evidence of an optimistic humanism.

One of the most interesting attempts at interpretation along these lines was done by the Catholic exegete, P. Benoit, in a series of articles on St. Paul, especially on the epistles of the captivity.[6] Fr. Benoit convincingly demonstrates that, as a general conclusion from these texts, we can say that Christ's redemptive power is not aimed exclusively (even though prin-

---

[5] Gustave Thils, *Christian Attitudes* (Chicago, 1959), pp. 90–92.
[6] P. Benoit, O.P., *Exegese et Théologie* (Paris, 1961), I, pp. 65–153.

cipally) at the salvation of men, but that it is also directed to the whole of the cosmos and the whole of reality which in some mysterious way will also share, through man, in redemption as it did in creation. One of the main difficulties along these lines has been the Platonic dualism, reinforced by Descartes and the Jansenists in more modern times, which has reigned in our theological textbooks. It was not always so, especially not for the biblical writers who say man is a whole, to be saved both in body and in soul. When, for example, St. Thomas set out to examine man in his *Summa Theologiae*, he called his study an investigation of man, not a treatise on the soul. Greek philosophy, in general, gave all attention to the soul; the body was regarded as its instrument, even its prison. In Greek thought, especially as reflected in Gnosticism and Manicheism, material reality, especially the body, was something evil or at least something to be got rid of, beginning in this life and fully liberated at death. Benoit even accuses some Catholic exegetes of misconceiving biblical thought in this fashion.

In our own day attention has been focused on the biblical anthropology according to which "body" is not a part of man opposed to the soul (Platonic dualism), but rather signifies all of man in his concrete actuality as a real person. This anthropology is certainly that of St. Paul, as many modern authors both Catholic and Protestant have been at pains to point out.[7]

Yet, as Fr. Pierre Charles has noted,[8] Platonic dualism is only one manifestation of a certain type of spirit which has infected not only Christianity but also every other religion of man. Twentieth-century materialism did not come about by chance. To a great degree it represents a reaction against the exaggerated theocratic society of the Middle Ages, where the subordination of the temporal to the spiritual was not one of dignity and finality, but rather one of servitude and direct subordination.

---

[7] L. Cerfaux, *Christ in the Theology of St. Paul* (New York, 1959), pp. 229–246; *Le Chrétien dans la théologie Paulinienne* (Paris, 1962), pp. 302–342.

[8] "Createur des chose visibles" in *l'Eglise: Sacrament du Monde* (Paris, 1960), pp. 57–73.

The reaction began in the Renaissance, but exclusive concentration on man and visible creation (the temporal) is a very recent development in the history of man. But to date, theologians have not met the problem on its own grounds. To decry materialism, atheism, secularism, socialism, etc., is all very fine, but beneath the whole question lies the rather ugly truth that Catholic theologians and philosophers have not really thought out the question in its total Christian perspective, where the supernatural-natural, sacred-profane are given their religious interpretation and orientation as *God wishes them to be seen.* In reality, Catholic theologians have for the most part taken the stand, with regard the temporal, either of an open pessimism (eschatology) and condemnation (all terrestrial realities are destined for fire and destruction in the "New Jerusalem") or else have held — and this is probably the most frequent attitude — that man's progress, history, and culture is much like the "basket-weaving" of the Middle Ages.[9] Other authors have already pointed out that this sort of thinking, although rather traditional (with a small "t"), does not seem to find much basis in the biblical texts. The eschatologists would erect a barrier between everyday human concerns and the things of the spirit; they would sever man's personal quest for salvation from all relationship with his social life. Yet is it not true that "Christian spirituality must not choose between an interior tendency and a social tendency, but in their extraodinary variety, all these forms are authentic and participate in each other"?[10] The Christian attitude is to face this grave problem for what it is and attempt to integrate both aspects into the totality of the Christian message. If our theological anthropology had been "integral" — especially since the later Middle Ages — there would be no overarching concern today to develop a theology of terrestrial realities. The words of St. Thomas are very true: *"All that man is, and what he can be and has, must be ordered*

---

9 J. Danielou, *The Lord of History* (Chicago, 1958).
10 H. DeLubac, *Catholicism* (London, 1956), pp. 206–207.

to God."[11] To say that music, art, society, international co-operation, harmony, and peace mean nothing for the Christian and for Christ is to contradict what each Christian feels in the depths of his heart. Such realities as common as work, technology, society of diverse types, the body and suffering must all be examined to determine their Christian meaning for modern man. Unless we can integrate these elements into our Christian *Weltanschauung*, we have profoundly lost all appeal and all contact with modern man. Then he must choose: himself or God.[12]

Earliest Attempts

As was already said, it is surprising, when we think of it, that the first condemnation of any doctrine in the history of Christianity was that of gnosticism, which taught a rather simple but heretical cosmogony or cosmic beginning. Gnosticism was characterized by a dualism between good and evil, a relegation of matter to evil, a philosophy that viewed terrestrial realities as chaotic and demonic. This gnostic vision of things was challenged by the fundamental formulation of our *Credo* at the Council of Nicea in 325. "I believe in one God . . . maker of heaven and of earth, of all things visible and invisible." This dogmatic truth was directed toward Christians within the Church — not to pagans. When one stops to realize its connotations, one sees that it is a tremendous thing. But creation is only half the story. In the words of Pierre Charles: "When you have defined the act of creation, it still remains to show with what new sense created things have been invested."[13] Since all things come from God, the unique Creator, to respect God and to respect the world cannot become two attitudes or tendencies which are divergent and between which we must

---

[11] *S.T.*, I–II, q. 21, a. 4, ad 3.
[12] Authors from the atheistic wing of existentialism give good descriptions of this. Cf. J. P. Sartre, *Being and Nothingness* (New York, 1956).
[13] P. Charles, *op. cit.*, p. 69.

choose. They are two solid and complementary aspects of the one and the same duty, of one love. It would indeed have shocked the gnostics of old to hear of Catholics celebrating such a feast as *Corpus Christi*. These notions must be recalled once in a while since, it seems, Catholics have a tendency to become Neoplatonic (gnostic) in the face of pain and suffering, sickness and death, and other difficult realities of man's life. It is all the more important today that theologians grapple with this problem inasmuch as progress in technology and science has given terrestrial things such a profound meaning for contemporary man.

The first contemporary attempts at a solution of this important problem go back to the beginning of the century with such men as Masure, Chamot, Maritain, Davenson, and Moehler. All of these authors, of course, came upon the scene toward the end of the past century, which had been one of progress and scientific evolution. Names like Pius IX, Pius X, Montalembert, Loisy, Darwin, Hegel, Marx, Dupanloup are all synonymous with the great struggle of the Church and the modern world of social and technical realities and revolution.[14] Their main object was to show that there was no inherent contradiction between Christianity and any true human value, be it social, artistic, or cultural. As a matter of fact, they argued, the human ideal found its completion only in the Christian who is the "full" man as God intended him to be.[15] They reacted and they intended to react against a theology which, as we have already pointed out, tended to be "spiritual" to an exaggerated degree, more Cartesian than Thomistic, which apparently had forgotten that matter, including all human values, is an indispensable element by which we proceed to the spiritual. These first works were more general in scope and did not descend into the basic particulars of life, v.g., work, progress, technology as such. In other words, the work of these fore-

---

[14] For an excellent brief summary, see E. E. Y. Hales, *The Catholic Church in the Modern World* (New York, 1958).

[15] See the magnificent pages in J. Maritain, *True Humanism* (London, 1958), pp. 288–304.

runners "was to create an idea according to which the Incarnation of the Son of God would be felt not only in the world of spirits but in the world of matter as well."[16] In the following chapters we shall see how later thinkers, relying on the solid bases established by Masure, Maritain, and others, have applied basic theological principles to specific questions of contemporary society.

---

[16] R. Aubert, *La Théologie au Milieu du XXe Siècle* (Tournai, 1954), pp. 62–63.

CHAPTER III

LATER THEOLOGICAL DEVELOPMENTS

Modern theologians, men like Scheler, Nedoncelle, Thils, Congar, Chenu, Dubarle, etc., have set about to give a theological analysis of such realities as the body, suffering, work, societies, technology, etc. Let us examine what they have to tell us.

Theology of Work

Probably one of the most remarkable theological developments in recent times has been that of a *theology* of work. It is all the more remarkable that we say *theology* of work and not the philosophy of work or the morality of work. The subject matter here is not at all recent, for the problem reaches back to the publication of Marx's *Das Kapital* more than a hundred years ago. Marx, of course, was not the first to see this problem nor was he the first thinker to give work serious consideration. But he was the first to make of work a systematic study and to produce, thereby, a true philosophy of work within the framework of the Hegelian dialectic of thesis, antithesis, and synthesis. His genius was to see the importance of work as a basic human value and drive, which is, in a sense, the very definition of man: *Homo oeconomicus*. Marx's genius, however, was intimately tied up with many erroneous social and metaphysical doctrines, and thus his system was necessarily rejected by Christian thinkers. A negative attitude toward ma-

26

terial things and "novel" opinions had been at work in Christian thought since the Council of Trent, and it was not until Leo XIII in 1891 (*Rerum Novarum*) and Pius XI in 1931 (*Quadragesimo Anno*) that we have any real attention paid to the Christian meaning of work.[1] But even with Leo and Pius concern centered on the conditions and rights of the worker rather than on the theological signification of work as a human reality. The phrase, "theology of work," is not over ten years old. Thus in the past few years, theologians have asked themselves whether, in the total plan of God, work has any intrinsic value in relationship to man's development as a creature, whether God endowed human labor with a special value at the moment of creation, without which man could not be a true and complete human being.

Theologians of the past have dwelt on the morality of work ("just wages for an honest day's work and vice versa") or have regarded labor as a duty of one's state of life whereby one earns daily bread both for himself and his family and in that way uses work as a means of sanctification.

Considerations of this kind are far from what we mean by a theology of work. Work is a reality which has its value independently of the worker's purpose or its use as a means of sanctification. A machine can indeed become for me a means of sanctification, and I can speculate on the morality of its use, its repercussions on society, etc. But that machine has been made by the builder for a specific purpose and end (*finis operis*) independently of the other "added" ends which it receives as the invention of human art and as a tool for human progress (*finis operantis*).

So, too, in a somewhat similar vein has the theology of work developed. Work is not an accessory or completely burdensome thing which is to be avoided whenever possible; on the con-

---

[1] Although valid as a general statement, this is not universally true. There have been some efforts to give a Christian interpretation of work from patristic times to the present. Nevertheless, it was only after the encyclical letters of Leo XIII and Pius XI that theologians took seriously their obligation to relate human work to the principles of faith.

trary, by work and its activity man finds his own perfection as the image of God who is to "dominate" all earthly creatures and develop their God-given potentialities. In Genesis we read that God created man "to his *image* and *likeness*." Commentators have long disputed the exact meaning of these two words, but in all probability the passage means that man, being God's lieutenant, must carry out His work of creation. On the seventh day God rested. His task of creation was finished; man's work had just begun.[2] Man is to complete this creation, to extend it in time and space according to the original intention of the Creator. The work, we read, of Adam in the garden of Eden was done before the fall — this clearly shows the error of those who claim that work is a result of sin or of the fall. On the contrary, for the author of this passage from Genesis, work is what makes man like God, at least in some way. Man is "defined" in terms of his "image and likeness" to God. His work will serve to bring out this image both in his own person and in the materials of creation on which he leaves his mark.

The original fall did not take this away, nor did the multitude of personal sins since. Work, however, was to become hard and painful (laborious), contrary to God's intentions for man. We have ample evidence for this throughout many of the books of the Old Testament.[3] Nevertheless, the biblical understanding of work was in direct contrast to the Greek disdain for manual labor and high esteem for leisure time — the *scholē* — in which only free men could participate. For the Hebrews, then, work was an honorable thing, and this probably as a result of the interpretation of Genesis.

In spite of the fact that Jesus Christ spent the majority of His life on earth as the "son of a carpenter," the impact of the biblical concept of work really came on the Christian mind only with Marx. Theologians now see work as a "creation" of man — or rather — a "humanization" of the world around us

---

[2] Here consult G. Thils, *Christian Holiness* (Tielt, 1961), p. 196.

[3] See Gn 24:1–30; Is 11:4; 42:1; Mk 6:3; etc.

from chaos to order, from a physical and brute reality to a human reality worthy of man to live in.[4] Man prolongs God's initial creation, to use Teilhard de Chardin's term, by a "hominization" of the world, that is, by taking over our planet from the brute forces of nature to which man has been a slave for thousands of years. This progress by work is man's business on earth. Certainly we do not define work in the sense that only physical labor can be work; more often than not, this is at the lowest scale of what true work is.[5] Compare in this regard the work of a brain surgeon, mending, ordering, healing, charged as it is with all the spiritual and intellectual skill involved in such an operation, and the work of a washerwoman. Both contribute to man's welfare, to order, to fulfillment of personalities, to the enrichment of the temporal order, but what a difference in degree of interiority and self-consciousness. "All artisans are engaged to restore all things in Christ by their work."[6] In brief, we can say with Fr. Ong, man's work "has made possible advances in communication which are essential to man's occupation of this planet, to man's taking over the planet from the forces of brute, non-intellectual nature."[7]

We do not neglect the dehumanizing elements of some forms of work (mechanization, chain work, etc.) concerning which a recent American book has given us ample warning.[8] But perhaps what is needed is a less negative approach, already well familiar to us, and a more positive and constructive attitude to the whole question.

Seen from a more positive and optimistic point of view, even

---

[4] W. Ong, "Technology and New Humanist Frontiers," in *Frontiers in American Catholicism* (New York, 1957), p. 88. Note also Teilhard de Chardin's notion of "hominization," which he develops in his *Phenomenon of Man* (New York, 1959).

[5] See the interesting observation of M. Merleau-Ponty that man's activity on matter is to bring it from "a natural situation to a cultured situation," *Sens et Non Sens* (Paris, 1940), p. 48; cf. the excellent remarks of L. J. Hall, "A Scholar-Priest's Vision of Man," *The New Republic*, 147 (Dec. 22, 1962), p. 20.

[6] Quoted by J. Cardinal D'Alton in a recent pastoral letter explaining the meaning of work (Chicago, September, 1960), p. 9.

[7] *Op. cit.*, p. 99.   [8] *Technology and Christian Culture* (Washington, 1960).

the "spirituality" of work takes on a new light. In cooperating with God in and through work, man fulfills God's work, for the supernatural will build well on what has been naturally well based; fraternal charity takes on a new light insofar as I, in helping and contributing to this common cause of "hominization," contribute my share to the health, safety, comfort, strength, and well-being of other men whom, perhaps, I shall never know but who are nonetheless all real. Nor are mortification and self-sacrifice left out of the picture, since the whole of work is simultaneously involved with monotony, laboriousness, sin, and self-profit. It becomes only too clear how a true asceticism of work could be developed by some spiritual writer. Work is man's instrument of liberation both from his egoism and his brute surroundings. Viewed in this way, work is no longer a brutal juxtaposition of individuals but a spiritual presence which, by a fraternal instinct, develops into a sort of social temperature never before felt.

And finally, in the words of Fr. Chenu, "There is the Incarnation. God became man and thus all becomes matter of grace. If work takes on a human consistence, it enters into the economy of grace; it enters twice as work of man and as a principle of the community which is also a land of grace. The Incarnation continued: *The Mystical Body of Christ, a thesis which will be henceforth classical in a spirituality where the world of work finds its equilibrium and its Christian place and is not simply regarded as an acquisition of merits.*"[9]

Theology of Human Values, Societies, Progress, and History

Such expressions as the "Christian notion of history," "the Christian sense of progress," "the Christian meaning of pain and of the body," have been getting abundant treatment of late. Studies on human love[10] have become commonplace in the recent revival of interest in the Sacrament of Matrimony. But

---

[9] M. P. Chenu, *Pour une Théologie du Travail* (Paris, 1955), p. 15.

[10] For example, the masterful work of J. Guitton, *Essay on Human Love* (London, 1953).

the interest in marriage is not the only reason for this study. The study of human love, of the body and its sacredness, is a study worthwhile in itself.[11] The body is a sign which expresses the meaning of the soul and its incarnation in matter. For there is absolutely no activity of man which does not involve the incarnate matter of his body. In this sense, men communicate by the sacredness of their bodies, expressing love and personality in and by them. The body is not something accessory to man but a part of his very definition. This is far from the Neoplatonism of former Jansenistic and puritanical centuries. In this sense, matter takes on its most sublime meaning as the instrument, extension, and expression of Spirit. The Incarnation of the Son of God, of course, is the main factor in all of these speculations on *homo, res sacra*. God became one of us, doubly sanctifying and consecrating what we are by associating our humanity with the flesh of His Son. At least that is the way the Greek Fathers used to picture the salvation of man: Christ physically touched our nature by becoming one with us in His human nature. Whatever we might think of the metaphors they used we cannot dispute the reality they were trying to convey: that man's human nature, his body as well as his soul, had been elevated to the heights of divine association and that just as Christ could no longer be separated from His human nature after His Resurrection — rather it reigns with Him in heaven — so too does the sacredness of our human nature proceed from our association with His.

The problem of pain and suffering has also come in for a great amount of research and study.[12] The argument from the existence of evil and pain in the world seems to be the most persuasive against belief in a personal Creator. Then, too, our own age has seen some of the most gruesome acts of sadism and cruelty since the dawn of history — at least in former times such deeds were not carried out in the cold, systematic way of

---

[11] See papal texts assembled in *The Body* (Boston, 1960). Also J. Mouroux, *The Meaning of Man* (New York, 1948).

[12] See especially C. S. Lewis, *The Problem of Pain* (London, 1940), and the recent work of Msgr. C. Journet, *The Meaning of Evil* (New York, 1963).

a Nazi concentration camp, of a Communist purge, or in the widespread obliteration bombings of innocent women and children. Add to this the precarious conditions in which our own world exists, under continuous threat of atomic or biological warfare, and we have a general "neurosis" and fear of the future. Can God see His children suffer and still be so hard as not to send them consolation or alleviation of their pain? If nothing else, any discussion of human suffering can be said to be packed with a certain emotionalism which is not made light of by theologians.

The problem of pain brings us to that of sickness and death, which has also witnessed some marvelous developments.[13] Is sickness exclusively a punishment of original sin? Most theologians hold that it is a result of sin, or at best a progressive weakening which eventually leads to death, which is certainly (de fide) a punishment of original sin. Entralgo here makes some interesting precisions and well-founded distinctions. Sickness is not necessarily a result of sin, for there could very well be another explanation — orthodox to be sure — which could fit into the Christian conception of man in his original state. Entralgo, for example, cites the words of our Lord to the man born blind: "Neither has this man sinned, nor his parents, but that the works of God might be manifest in him" and goes on to point out the examples of Job and of Mary, who suffered much pain, yet were not sinners. He concludes from these reflections that sickness is not necessarily a result of sin, but that it could well be an integral feature of the mystery of suffering of the human person, a means God uses to draw us closer to Himself. This original insight of Entralgo certainly gives the Christian much food for thought when he contemplates the sometimes terrible sea of suffering and pain around him.

And what of the development of progress and of technology

---

[13] See the enlightening study of Pedro L. Entralgo, "Essay for a Theology of Illness," in Faith, Reason, and Modern Psychiatry (New York, 1956), pp. 207–243. Cf. K. Rahner, Toward a Theology of Death (New York, 1962).

in particular?[14] The essential word to be used here is *liberation*. Technology and science have helped free men from the slaveries and fears of millions of years: disease, the elements, wild life, etc. All these forces man has now learned to dominate, control, and use, whereas before, so we are told, he was left to the mercy of God or the gods.[15] To this latter conclusion, there is only one small jump and it is a jump which many of our contemporary humanists have already made. Arguing along these lines, such thinkers hold that God and divine revelation are relics of a primitive, naïve epoch of man's history. Today they should be regarded as "myth." Thus, the importance for the Catholic theologian to give some orientation to the progress of science, medicine, technology, etc., in the course of history. But can this be done in the present context of revelation? This is the question which has preoccupied theologians for some time now.

We have already seen that a whole group of Catholic theologians refuses to grant any real, intrinsic value either to history or to progress. At the head of this group and certainly its most prominent member is the French Jesuit, Jean Danielou. He wrote:

> For the Christian, the world of natural life and science, the world of the temporal city and of economic life is something essentially achronistic. It is radically overshadowed by the world of the Church which is its future already present. The world of the Church in its own term appears with relation to the political society as "catachronic," that is to say, the anticipation of a reality

---

[14] See the outstanding works of C. Dawson, *Medieval Essays* (New York, 1959); *Progress and Religion* (New York, 1960); *Understanding Europe* (New York, 1960). His latest book deals with the specific problem of the relationship of Christianity and education taken in its total context of general culture: *The Crisis of Western Education* (New York, 1961).

[15] This seems to be the argument proposed by many men of science today. As long as man remained in the metaphysical, he had to depend on external, "supernatural" help. Now man has learned to use his inherent natural powers of reason and has so destroyed the God who, in reality, was none other than himself. At least so argued Feuerbach in his *Homo homini Deus*. Early attempts by Catholic men of science to disprove this can be seen in the marvelous book of Lecomte du Nouey, *Human Destiny* (New York, 1947). In our own day, Pierre de Chardin has brought this to even a sharper focus in *The Phenomenon of Man* (New York, 1959) and *The Divine Milieu* (New York, 1960).

to appear in the measure that it pertains to the future. Juxtaposition of a past and a present, such is the Christian present.[16]

For others, those who call themselves the "Incarnationalists," all this most certainly does have a sense. Their feelings are summed up in the words of P. Malvez: "If these views are correct, then it follows that, taken in itself, the contemporary mastery over matter, political organization, art, thought and all technology, completes Christ and in completing Him glorifies Him. They would do this no matter what the intention, pure or perverse, which animates the man who does them. . . . This result announces and inaugurates the consummation of the Mystical Body of the God-man."[17]

This indeed appeals both to modern man and to an integrated Christianity. Evolution no longer seems to be inimical to Christianity, quite the contrary. Due to the efforts of Pierre Teilhard de Chardin, evolution has even led to a more profound Christian understanding of the entire cosmos inclusive of the "noosphere." The potentialities of God, then, are understood to expand themselves in wondrous fashion over the billions and millions of years of the existence of the cosmos. Chardin sees this as finally culminating in the social unification of "Omega Point" — which is this evolution consciously and lovingly evolved. "Try, with God's help, to perceive the connection — even physical and natural — which binds your labour with the building of the kingdom of Heaven."[18] We have come quite a long way from Loisy and his companions who found in the notion of evolution the stumbling block for Christianity.

But can we really discern any positive direction to, say, the course of history (the philosophy and theology of history) or, again, to the progress of science and technology in relation to the kingdom? This indeed is one of the chief problems of modern theologians. From revelation we know that the whole

[16] "Christianisme et Histoire," *Etudes*, 282 (1947), 182–183.
[17] "La Philosophie Chrétienne du Progrès," *Nou. Rev. Théo.*, 64 (1937), 377–385.
[18] *The Divine Milieu*, p. 35.

of history is dominated by the Holy Spirit who continuously "spiritualizes" the events in history and in the whole of human realities. But what does "spiritualizing" mean? For a clear understanding of this work in the Holy Spirit we must go to the epistles of St. Paul which we have, however, already examined.[19] Are there any general observations and theological conclusions we can draw from our biblical-theological analysis of this problem? It is to these matters that we now turn.

---

[19] *Supra*, pp. 20–21; see among the texts of St. Paul: Col 1:9; 1 Cor 2:15; Eph 5:19; 1 Cor 15:44; Gal 5:19–21; 2 Cor 1:2.

CHAPTER IV

THE THEOLOGY OF HISTORY AND TECHNOLOGY

History

FEW historians are agreed on the definition of history itself. Depending on one's philosophical prejudices, one will have a notion of history which is either spiritualistic or materialistic or pantheistic, etc. Perhaps the best definition from a Christian point of view is that of Fr. Danielou: "A reality continuous and discontinuous at the same time, where there is, between the past and the future, both a true qualitative difference and an ensemble of correspondences and prefigurations."[1] This definition makes a lot of sense when one has accepted the historical reality of the Incarnation of the Son of God. Without that essential element, the Christian conception of history becomes a Promethean myth. We shall return to this definition of Fr. Danielou later.

A first observation is that Christianity, and Christianity alone, offers a true meaning to history. Many studies have been made of the Greek, Hindu, Buddhist, etc., conceptions of history (see the studies of Thils, De Lubac, M. Montuchard, Davidson, Cullmann, and others). The Greek theory, so well analyzed by O. Cullmann in his marvelous book *Christ and Time*, was one of eternally recurring circles. After millions of years, the same thing was bound to occur again and again, for history had no end, no finality, no *telos*; it was the eternal pessimism and

---

[1] *The Lord of History* (Chicago, 1960), p. 24.

despair so common to Greek writers before Christ. Plato himself, or at least Plato as interpreted by his disciples, had only the solution of *escape* from the world of time to the world of immutable ideas and essences; his concept was not a solution, but an escape from the realities of time and space. So too with the religions of the East outside of Judaism (and later, Christianity). They are all, without exception, attitudes of escape and evasion from the difficult aspects of reality. Thus, the well-being of the Buddhists, the nirvana of the Hindus, the materialism of the Epicureans are all variants of an escapist mind set.

If the world today possesses an authentic idea of history, then it owes it to Christianity. At a certain period in time, God made His entrance into the world of flesh and blood, *factum ex muliere*. From that time on, history has received a sense, a value; for who says end and finality also says sense and value. Christ has come and He will come again; we are already engaged in the eschatological times in which we have received the token of the Spirit. The kingdom is already present in seed. The final consummation is still awaited but, in the words of Newman, "If He tarry, He will surely come." Christ is the center, the means, and the end; He has given history a definitive meaning for the Christian in a true theological sense.

That is why other interpretations of history are either incomplete or unsatisfying for the deep-seated instincts of man. In the words of Fr. De Lubac:

> Christianity alone affirms for man a transcendent destiny and for humanity as such, a common destiny. All history in the world is a preparation for that destiny. From creation to the final consummation, through all the resistance of matter and of the free will of man, the same divine will will be fulfilled. . . . *Circuitus illi jam explosi sunt.* It is the triumphal cry of the Christian to whom God has been revealed as Creator and Saviour. The infernal circle of the Greeks has been destroyed. Historical facts are no longer just single phenomena, they have become events, acts, *gesta Dei*. There is a birth, an effective growth, a maturing of the universe. The world having an end,

has therefore a sense, i.e., a direction and a signification. The whole human race is the child of God and all is sustained within the hands of God, and in the word by the Spirit, all is directed to the Father.[2]

We rather think that without this basic presupposition it is difficult if not altogether impossible to give any sense, even philosophical, to the history of mankind. The Greeks failed because they could see no way to break out of the chain of eternal return; the Eastern religions because of their evasion and escape; materialism because of its failure to take cognizance of the total reality of man as body and spirit.

A second observation to be made within the orbit of Christian thought is the meaning of diverse civilizations in history. In other words, do the diverse civilizations in which Christianity has incarnated itself, and some of which have already disappeared, have any real, intrinsic meaning for Christ and Christianity? Or are they, in the words of Fr. Danielou, mere vestments to be put on by Christianity and to be cast off when it no longer has any use of them? In his own words: "Christian civilizations are always transitory and corruptible; the Church must, after having worn them for a time, throw them off like old vestments."[3] Fr. Danielou, as we have seen, is one of the leading eschatologists, who see in human culture and civilization no meaning for the kingdom. When Christ comes in glory (parousia) to establish the kingdom in its definitive stage, all these aspects of history, of civilization and culture will be done away with because "the figure of this world has passed."

We have previously noted that this school of thought has not sufficiently taken into consideration the incarnational aspect of Christianity. Is it true that none of the historical realities of man have any meaning for Christ? This we consider one of the major points for thought among Christian thinkers. There are, indeed, passages in Scripture which would seem to point in

---

[2] Catholicism (London, 1955), p. 70; St. Augustine, De Civitate Dei, 12, c. 20, n. 4 (P.L. 41, 371); Isidor of Seville, De Ordine Creaturarum, c. 11, n. 6 (P.L. 83, 943); St. Ambrose, In Lukam (P.L. 15, c. 1745), etc.

[3] Danielou, op. cit., p. 64.

another direction than that of the total view of Fr. Danielou: the humanity of Christ, our own resurrected bodies, the *Dormitio* of the Blessed Virgin, the matter of the Sacraments themselves are all signs that perhaps some elements of a civilization or culture do continue and will continue to exist after the definitive establishment of the kingdom itself by Christ. In any case, it would seem to be a very serious and important problem, especially for those who are actively engaged in the building of the *cosmopolis* of our own day, particularly laymen. It certainly makes a lot of difference to them whether their life's work and sweat have an intrinsic meaning or are destined for total destruction. It could almost be said that this is the most important problem facing Christian historical scholars.[4]

Science and Technology

The terms *science* and *technology* are certainly not the same. Science is habitually used in a much broader sense to include all of the pure and applied sciences while technology is used almost exclusively to mean the practical applied sciences alone. In our present context, the two terms are used indiscriminately since the so-called "common man," when he speaks of them, means the same thing.

This problem more than any other is peculiar to modern man. The development in the sciences during the past 200 years has far outstripped the combined advances of mankind in all previous history. It has affected man not only in a quantitative measure (more facility of travel, better conditions, etc.) but to an even larger degree in a qualitative measure. Four main observations, we believe, are in order with regard to the qualitative effects of technology.

1. With the more perfect technology developed over the space of recent years, servile work ("slavery" to work as some

[4] This was certainly one of the main preoccupations of some of the authors of articles contained in *The Intent of Toynbee's History* (New York, 1961). See also A. Schweitzer, *The Philosophy of Civilization* (New York, 1960), for a non-Catholic interpretation.

theologians call it) has been constantly reduced. Man is no longer the slave to nature's whims (draughts, floods, insects, etc.) in his efforts to transform nature. Science has thus permitted the more spiritual aspects of man to develop freely, if not always *de facto*, since, even here, men reserve their option of free will.

2. Through the advance of the social sciences, it has become more and more possible to regulate as well as dominate the course of social events: "socialization" at its best in its moderate forms (*cf.* the recent encyclical, *Mater et Magistra*), organization of insurances, unemployment benefits, just distribution of quantitative taxes, etc. This aspect of the social sciences is an indispensable factor in making the benefits of technology accessible to the great majority of the people in a particular civilization.

3. Augmentation of productivity permits modern civilization to work effectively and with a definite method for the suppression of enormous inequalities, both economic and social. The possibility is at our disposal to eliminate or at least to alleviate to a large degree the so-called "underdeveloped" countries of the world. Never before in history has this possibility been ours. Pius XII and John XXIII have pointed out the fact that most nations have the possibility of self-sufficiency if they can only develop and evenly distribute and exchange (trade) their enormous, untouched resources. We of the West with our superior technological advances are in a position to aid them. This indeed is one of the great dramas of our time: technology and economic development.

4. As a result of the above, for the first time in history, all men can truly collaborate in mastering nature and in advancing truly human goals. The future generations as well as the present must turn their thoughts from a narrow nationalism, self-centered history and concern to the international (interplanetary?) scene more and more. "International responsibility" is no longer a high-sounding moral phrase; it is a definitive fact already acquired in certain realms (think of the UN and the

great work of its subsidiary organizations, such as UNESCO, WHO, etc.). Technology has brought about the era of a humanity which is truly and effectively universal. A common life in which all share has made us more and more a cosmopolitan and even cosmic civilization.

One cannot, however, deny the inherent drawbacks of technology and science as we know them today. These difficulties are cited because they continue to cause much worry to Catholic thinkers on this subject, almost to the point of obsession. Witness, for example, the rather negative approach to this problem by a symposium recently carried on under the auspices of the Catholic University of America: *Technology and the Christian.* Let us observe that:

1. It does not automatically follow that technological progress necessarily means a perfection of man. It can help by liberating man from the slavery of want, disease, but at the same time can lead to a dissipation of leisure time in meaningless activity that is so common among Americans.[5]

2. Technology and science, in a sense, are, in the words of Niebuhr, ambiguous in themselves. They can be used for great good (think of the tremendous good which could come from the Telstar) or turned to great evil (think of Hiroshima, etc.). Unless Christians attempt to influence the current of thought along the lines of good, there is little hope that any satisfactory solution will be found.

3. Such a progress easily leads to materialism. What was done before by prayer is done now by medicine. "Religion is the opium of the people." Much Christian thinking has given the enemy occasion for such accusation. The true Christian thinker versed in both religion and technology can serve to

---

[5] See the popular sociological studies of D. Reisman and others, *The Lonely Crowd* (New York, 1953); B. Russell, *The Impact of Science on Society* (New York, 1951); P. Sorokin, *Social and Cultural Dynamics* (New York, 1937–1941); E. H. Spicer, *Human Problems in Technological Change* (New York, 1952); W. Whyte, *The Organization Man* (New York, 1956); A. Dondyne, "Technology and Religion," *Albertus Magnus*, 6, 4–9; G. Friedmann, "Technological Change and Human Relations," *Cross Currents*, 10 (1960), 29–47.

prove the great lie of their incompatibility. There is indeed great need of a modern apologetic.

4. Our society has tended to make men strangers to each other and slaves to the technological system (one thinks here of the *organization man*) as individual cogs in administrative machinery. This is a problem which has afflicted our technological society as a *whole* (even the Church) and more thought must be given to this problem by theologians and sociologists alike.

And, finally, cannot the progress of science and technology itself be a liberating force for man, a prefiguration or prelude of the coming of the kingdom? Cannot international trade agreements serve as foretastes of the harmony, peace, and, above all, of the fraternal love in sharing, as a figure of spiritual goods, the material goods necessary for a decent human existence? And cannot there be a definitive theological interpretation of automation (with all its drawbacks) as a means whereby man is freed to perform more human tasks, work more in conformity with his noble vocation as *artifex*, impregnating matter and leading it toward what it will be definitively under the supreme eschatological work of the great *Artifex* who is Christ? Here is what even a man of the world has to say about this: "The liberation of people from tasks unworthy of human capacity should free that capacity for a host of activities now neglected in our civilization: teaching and learning, fundamental scientific investigation, the performing arts and graphic arts, letters, the crafts, politics and social science. Characteristically these activities involve the interaction of people rather than things."[6]

Certainly we cannot eliminate the cross from this perhaps too optimistic view of the elaboration of the temporal order under the inspiration of the Holy Spirit. The historical sequence is not always a forward-moving sequence; it has its backslidings, its failures, its drawbacks; but the Christian should not, and

---

[6] G. Piel, *Consumers of Abundance* (an occasional paper on the role of economic order, published by the Center for the Study of Democratic Institutions, 1961), p. 9.

must not, become discouraged. Perhaps these very setbacks will be an occasion, providential perhaps, for purification of intention, renewal of purpose, and dedication for Christ and for men, *instaurare omnia in Christo*. In the wise words of Fr. Thils:

> But if we have faith in the total efficacy (supernatural and natural) of the Spirit, if we believe that God is more powerful than Satan, if we admit that the grace of Christ is more abundant than the sin of Adam, we can estimate that the weight of good realized in the world by the Holy Spirit will be dominant, that it will even grow without suppressing the reactions and oppositions of man and the devil, taking the ensemble of men, by ways and detours, toward a greater organic unity, universality, a greater peace, more liberty and even greater sanctity.[7]

Conclusion

This part has already passed the bounds intended. Yet we have not touched all points involved in the gigantic study now wide open for Catholic thought. Never before in history has so much material for speculation as to its theological meaning been waiting for some answer, sometimes an agonizing waiting, for its finality and purpose. Only Christianity can give it hope of that answer. Every other religion is radically incapable of such a theological endeavor because of some basic incompatibility with its own internal structure: the Eastern religions because of their denial either of matter itself or of its positive value; materialism and Communism because of their denial of a substantial soul. Then must the men of our day despair? The responsibility of this great theological question will depend very much on an integral Christian theological synthesis which is and can be the only authentic answer. The etchings of a solution have already started to appear in Catholic theological circles. Since time waits for no one, it is more imperative than ever that Catholic thought grapple with this problem in an age which longs for a "substantial soul" for its history, progress, technology, and human

---

[7] G. Thils, *Théologie et realité sociale* (Tournai, 1952), p. 300.

values. Only future historians will be able to say whether we shall have helped solve the problem or negated it by ignoring it. In that proportion will future historians either commend or condemn us. The responsibility is a heavy one, but the challenge is too great to be avoided.

Bibliographical Note

The bibliography we have already is quite abundant. Yet there still remains a general orientation to the literature in this vast field which can be given to the reader. He will find in the books themselves abundant reference to continue his study if he wishes.

1. Allen, Francis, and others. *Technology and Social Change.* New York: Appleton-Century-Crofts, 1957.

   A valuable contribution for seeing the effect of modern technology on the diverse elements in society, particularly the family and work. Allen points out the value of technology but is at pains to show, above all, the change with social structures of the past.

2. Arendt, Hannah. *The Human Condition.* Garden City, New York: Doubleday Anchor Books, 1959.

   An interesting work from the point of view of Arendt's emphasis on contemplation. Perhaps somewhat exaggerated; it seems to fail in the application of principles to all types of work as leading to some type of contemplation, to some extent at least, if not all in the same degree.

3. Bennett, John C., and others. *Christian Values and Economic Life.* New York: Harper and Bros., 1954.

   An interesting attempt from a non-Catholic point of view to draw Christian implications from economic life. What is important to note here is that these values are not "aside" the Christian life but intimately implied in it for man.

4. Borne, Et., and Henry, F. *A Philosophy of Work.* London: Sheed and Ward, 1938.

   One of the earliest attempts to develop a philosophy of work in all its ramifications. As such, it is an excellent starting point, but there still remains, perhaps, an exaggerated reaction against the Marxian interpretation with no attempt to draw the good from that system.

5. Bouyer, Louis. *Christian Humanism.* New York: Macmillan Co., 1960.

A short work which attempts to give justification to a certain type of humanism which can be called Christian in a proper sense. It is interesting to note Bouyer's attempt, since he is an "eschatologist" in the sense explained in the text.

6. Chase, Sh. J. *The Christian Philosophy of History*. Chicago, Ill.: Chicago University Press, 1943.

Magnificent from the point of view of bibliography, of which this author is in complete control. After tracing the solutions which have been given to the problem, he proceeds to draw some of his own conclusions. His "Christian" philosophy is obviously that of Protestant Christianity, but his points are very well taken.

7. Chenu, M. D. *Pour une Théologie du Travail*. Paris: Ed. de Seuil, 1955.

A very small work which is worth its weight in gold. Chenu attempts to view work in the context of Scripture and theology. Starting from the fact of initial creation given to man, he analyzes the potentialities brought out by man's work.

8. Congar, Yves. *Laity, Church and World*. Baltimore: Helicon Press, 1960.

9. ———— *Lay People in the Church*. Westminster, Md.: The Newman Press, 1957.

Two fundamental works on the lay apostolate. Since the latter is concerned with the temporary properly speaking, Congar devotes considerable length to a theological and religious elaboration on the temporal realities of man (history, culture, work, etc.). Of particular interest are his definitions of the redemption of Christ as extended to all of reality *de jure* and *de facto*, and his remarks on the layman's duties to Christ.

10. Considine, J., ed. *The Missionary's Role in Socio-Economic Betterment*. Westminster, Md.: Newman Press, 1960.

It is Considine's contention that the temporal betterment of the peoples to whom missionaries are sent is extremely important in our day and age. Therefore, he attempts to show the reason for this and its worth within the Christian context of temporal realities.

11. Cronin, John F. *Social Principles and Economic Life*. Milwaukee: Bruce Pub. Co., 1959.

Basic text used in many Catholic schools. Particularly emphasized is the growing concern of the Popes over social justice in the temporal order and the signification of the latter in Christian life. Cronin attempts to show that the temporal is of equal importance to the "spiritual" in an integral Christian life.

12. Cullmann, O. *Christ and Time*. Philadelphia: Westminster, 1950.

What does time mean for the Christian? The Greeks conceive of it as history repeating itself in an eternal circle or recurrence. For the Christian, however, time is redemptive (and therefore history) since it has received a beginning and an end in Christ.

13. Danielou, J. *The Lord of History.* Chicago: Henry Regnery, 1958.

A Catholic master in the field gives here a compilation of various articles written over the years. As an "eschatologist," he sees human culture as useful for the work of Christianity, but argues that it must be totally destroyed in the end.

14. D'Arcy, M. C. *The Meaning and Matter of History.* New York: Farrar, Straus and Cudahy, 1959.

Probably the most successful work on this subject in Catholic circles. The reading is difficult but rewarding. Fundamentally, the author sees a definite trend in history toward a fuller Christianization of the progress of history with various setbacks.

15. Davenson, M. H. *Fondements d'une Culture Chrétienne.* (Col. Cahiers de la Nouvelle Journée) Paris: Bloud et Gay, 1934.

Does culture (music, art, technology, etc.) have any real and basic signification for the Christian? Yes, answers Davenson, by showing how they can fit into the Christian scheme of revelation and theology. He proceeds to give the basic elements which are necessary if one wants to speak of a "Christian culture" properly so called.

16. Dawson, Christopher. *The Crisis of Western Education.* New York: Sheed and Ward, 1961.

17. ———— *Medieval Essays.* Garden City, N. Y.: Image Books, 1959.

18. ———— *Progress and Religion.* Garden City, N. Y.: Image Books, 1960.

19. ———— *Religion and the Rise of Western Culture.* Garden City, N. Y.: Image Books, 1958.

20. ———— *Understanding Europe.* Garden City, N. Y.: Image Books, 1960.

21. ———— *The Dynamics of World History.* New York: Mentor Omega Books, 1962.

All of the works are absolutely necessary if one is to understand anything of Western culture and Christianity's influence upon it. What is the "cadre" into which Christianity can fit, and how has it done this in our own Western and European culture? What are its lasting values and meaning for us today, or the men of tomorrow?

22. De Lubac, H. *Catholicism.* London: Burns and Oates, 1949.

23. ———— *Surnaturel.* (Coll. "Théologie"), Paris: Aubier, 1946.

Both works are essential for a comprehension of the vital relations between the natural and supernatural orders. This is a vital question in any theology of terrestrial realities.

24. Demant, V. A. *Theology of Society*. London, 1947.

One of the first attempts to determine the presuppositions and requirements for any Christian conception of society. Social justice, peace, etc., are discussed from a Christian point of view.

25. De Montcheuil, Y. *Guide to Social Action*. Chicago: Fides, 1956.

Various essays on the duty of the Christian in all phases of the temporal order: politics, business, Church-State relations, etc. Very interesting is De Montcheuil's view of the relationship between the temporal and the sacred, properly speaking.

26. Donahue, J. W. *Work and Education*. Chicago: Loyola University Press, 1959.

A series of essays on the nature and orientation of work and its Christian meaning. It has the merit of being one of the few discussions in English on this subject. An excellent bibliographical note adds to its value.

27. Dubarle, D. *Optimisme devant Ce Monde*. Paris: Ed. du Cerf, 1949.

A very stimulating book for biblical and theological connotations of creation and man's work upon it. Dubarle concludes that man's primary job as man is to develop all the potentialities given him in creation. This gives man a certain optimism as regards the future of progress, etc.

28. Dupreel, E. *Deux Essais sur le Progres*. Bruxelles: M. La Mertin, 1928.

The author tries to analyze the direction of modern progress to see whether there is any Christian interpretation which can be given to it. In particular, the orientations of technology and science are given a full coverage.

29. Frank-Duquesne, Albert. *Cosmos et Gloire*. Paris: Librarie Philosophique J. Vrin, 1947.

A rather mystifying but helpful work insofar as the author attempts to see all the divine ramifications in the whole universe, physical, psychological, and spiritual. The approach is from an Eastern mystical point of view.

30. Gilson, E. *The Christian Philosophy of St. Augustine*. New York: Random House, 1960.

31. ———— *The Spirit of Medieval Philosophy*. New York: C. Scribner, 1946.

Both of these works are important for a setting of the Augustinian and medieval syntheses of the relation of the Christian to the temporal. St. Augustine was one of the first writers to envision such a scope, and his thought permeated the discussions of later medieval theologians.

32. Greeley, Andrew. *The Church and the Suburbs*. New York: Sheed and Ward, 1959.

A representative work on the relation between the Church and modern civilization in general. The author sees a great change in the mentality of modern man because of the revolutionary character of modern technological society. No real solution given; the problem is simply posed.

33. Guardini, R. *The End of the Modern World*. New York: Sheed and Ward, 1956.

Guardini attempts to focus our attention on approximately the same problem as posed in Greeley's work: modern man, technological and industrialized society, and the faith. What is the solution?

34. Guellery, K. *Le Travail dans la vie du Chrétien*. Grembloux: Duculot, 1953.

The author attempts to integrate the notion of work (in all of its ramifications) into the total Christian interpretation of reality. Some interesting observations especially on creation as continued by man.

35. Hamain L. *Realités Terrestres et vie Chrétienne*. These de doctorat en Theologie. (Lille), 1959. 2 vols.

A doctoral dissertation which attempts to sum up all of Christian as well as pagan thought on the relationship of man to created reality and to God. Very good for bibliographical information and guides.

36. Humman, A. *La Redemption et L'Ordre Social Chrétien*. Paris: Plon, 1949.

How is the social order specifically Christian, or can it be at all? What are the general conditions which must be fulfilled to bring about such an order? The author attempts to show how social values are, in reality, very Christian values.

37. Hoyland, J. S. *Faith and History*. London: S.C.M. Press, 1926.

A rather superficial but popular study of the relation between Christian faith and history in general. The author contends that throughout the past 2000 years, Christianity has definitely been not only an influencing factor but a directing force in history.

38. Huby, Joseph. *Saint Paul. Epitre Aux Romains*. Paris: Beauchesne, 1957.

Cited because of its cosmological interpretation of Romans 8:16.

The author claims that Catholics are too restrictive of Pauline soteriology which must be extended not only to souls, but to the totality of the cosmos.

39. Jaspers, Karl. *Man in the Modern Age.* Garden City, New York: Doubleday Anchor Books, 1957.

Diverse essays on the specific problems of man in our age. Among these, especially important for the Christian, is the problem and confrontation of faith with the modern and scientific world of today.

40. Journet, Ch. *Exigences Chrétiennes et Politique.* Paris: Desclée, 1945.

Journet attempts to show the Christian meaning of the political order. It is not, claims the author, a result of sin but a demand of man's nature. Therefore, the Christian must include this order in his *Weltanschauung.*

41. Loewith, K. *Meaning in History: The Theological Implications of the Philosophy of History.* Chicago: Chicago University Press, 1948.

The direction of history is not only a philosophical question but also one of theology. As such, it lends itself to theological speculation. The author attempts to draw some theological conclusions from this philosophy.

42. Lagarde, George. *La Naissance de L'Esprit Laique.* Louvain: Ed. Nauwelaerts, 1956. 6 vols.

Ever since the latter medieval period, there has been a continuous separation of the religious from the secular, properly speaking. The author attempts to show what were the factors involved which led to this lamentable situation.

43. Leclercq, Jacques. *The Christian Before Money.* New York: Hawthorn Books, 1960.

Money is only symbolical of the temporal as such. Fr. Leclercq attempts to give in popular form and in a few pages the Christian attitude toward the material reality in which men must work out their salvation.

44. Leclercq, Jean. *The Love of Learning and the Desire for God.* New York: Mentor Omega Books, 1962.

Learning is not a superfluous addition to man's nature. Fundamentally, all knowledge is but a reflection of the Divine Creation and a real participation in the knowledge of God. Knowledge is here taken to mean what it signifies in the Bible: intellect and engagement.

45. Lorson, P. *Le Plaisir Sanctifié: Pour une Spiritualité des Loisirs.* Colmar: Alsatia, 1952.

Leisure is not an escape; it is but the other side of work and must be used constructively to build up one's personality and interests. The author claims that modern technology has given man more leisure but that, reversely, this must be used profitably. He gives some specific solutions.

46. Lossky, V. *The Mystical Theology of the Eastern Church*. London: James Clarke, 1957.

A very interesting study on the way the Eastern Church includes and utilizes the totality of the material universe as a reflection of the Uncreated, especially in the liturgy.

47. Lynch, William. *The Image Industries*. New York: Sheed and Ward, 1959.

48. ———— *Christ and Apollo*. New York: Sheed and Ward, 1960.

Two works by a native American which study the creative imagination in art, movies, etc., as reproducing the real image of man created in God's likeness. Very valuable for the modern world and Christian entertainment and art.

49. Maritain, J. *Art and Scholasticism*. New York: Charles Scribner, 1957.

50. ———— *On the Philosophy of History*. New York: Charles Scribner, 1957.

51. ———— *True Humanism*. New York: Charles Scribner, 1954.

52. ———— *Ransoming the Time*. New York: Charles Scribner, 1957.

Maritain's works are some of the first attempts to justify a Christian humanism. The author claims in these diverse works that only the Christian can bring to full blossom all the potentialities of creation, in the full sense. Time, art, culture, history, all have a basic meaning in the Christian message.

53. Masure, E. *L'Humanisme Chrétien*. Paris, 1937.

Similar to Maritain, the author justifies a Christian interpretation of all creation in and through man. Since all was created for man and through man, for Christ, we should be able to see their images therein.

54. Mead, Margaret, ed. *Cultural Patterns and Technical Change*. New York: New American Library, 1955.

Rather pessimistic in outlook, this book deals with changing cultural patterns as effects of modern technology. The author attempts to show what is nonchanging in function of what has changed.

55. Moeller, C. *Humanisme et Sainteté*. Tournai-Paris: Casterman, 1949.

Humanism not only reflects God's image, but it also sanctifies those who work at it with this intention. But how to gain this intention? By first seeing the Christian sense of the temporal and created orders.

56. Mohan, R. P., ed. *Technology and Christian Culture*. Washington, D. C.: The Catholic University of America Press, 1960.

A series of essays mostly on the drawbacks and the dangers of modern technology. What is most dissatisfying is the essay on the Mystical Body and technology. The approach is negative with few attempts to integrate the positive side of technology into the Christian picture of things.

57. Monzel, N. *Die Soziologie und die Theologie*. Hochland, 1949.

The author studies the relationship between these two sciences and the means for integrating them into one complete system. The author says that we must distinguish Christian principles from their application.

58. Mouroux, J. *The Meaning of Man*. New York: Sheed and Ward, 1948. Image Books, 1961.

A series of well-done essays on the material universe, the body, love, progress, etc., within the framework of a Christian setting. The author points out the relationship of these to the kingdom of Christ.

59. Murphy, S. E., ed. *Christianity and Culture*. Baltimore: Helicon Press, 1960.

Various essays by different authors on the relationship of culture (which includes art, history, technology, etc.) to Christianity. Very rewarding reading but at times a bit too superficial.

60. Murray, J. C. *We Hold These Truths*. New York: Sheed and Ward, 1960.

A powerful book on the relationship of the secular and religious orders (as well as Church and state). The function of legal legislation is also clearly described; one could call the book an essay on the relationship of the Christian to the political order.

61. Niebuhr, H. R. *Christ and Culture*. New York: Harper Brothers, 1951.

From a Protestant point of view, the author gives a balanced view on the relationship of the Christian to created reality of all types. The author is rather pessimistic concerning the future of man's labor and progress.

62. Ong, Walter. *American Catholic Crossroads*. New York: Macmillan Co., 1959.

63. ———— *Frontiers in American Catholicism*. New York: Macmillan Co., 1957.

Individual considerations of the problems of the American Catholic today. Since the latter lives in a highly technological and business society, Ong examines the modern world for meaning and Christian interpretation. The business world and technology are examined with profitable insight for others.

64. Ogburn, William. *Social Change with Respect to Culture and Original Nature.* New York: Viking Press, 1922.

65. ———— *Technology and the Changing Family.* Boston: Houghton Mifflin Co., 1955.

The author examines the influence of modern technology on social change and adaptation. The second book is of particular interest to evolving patterns of family life in our modern societies. The author's notions, however, on "original" nature are hazy indeed.

66. Packard, Vance. *The Hidden Persuaders.* New York: McKay Co., 1957.

67. ———— *The Status Seekers.* New York: McKay Co., 1959.

Popular sociology in paperback form but useful for finding the frame of mind of our compatriots living in the modern world, their sense of values, etc. This is good source material for viewing some of the drawbacks of a highly mobile and industrial society.

68. Pieper, J. *The End of Time.* New York: Pantheon Books, 1954.

Along with Professor Cullmann, Pieper attempts to show the Christian meaning of time. Time for the Christian is not an empty "pastime" but a redemptive value from Christ who is the center of time. Time — and all the temporal — becomes a prolongation of Christ by man.

69. Pius XII, Pope. *The Function of Art.* Address of Pope Pius XII on Sacred Art. Washington, D. C.: NCWC, 1952.

70. ———— *Films, Radio and TV.* Encyclical of Pius XII. New York: The America Press, 1957.

71. ———— *The Human Body.* Selected and arranged by the Monks of Solesmes. Boston: St. Paul editions, 1960.

As was said in the body of the paper, this Holy Father was intensely interested in the temporal for its "spiritual" and human values. It is interesting to note how much material has been consecrated to this subject.

72. Renard, G. *Life and Work in Prehistoric Times.* New York: Knopf, 1929.

This is a general history of the notion of work from the earliest times of recorded history. It is interesting to note the diverse religious interpretations which were given to it by various ancient tribes.

73. Rideau, E. *Consécration de Christianisme et L'Activité Humaine.* Paris: Desclée, 1945.

The author attempts to show the Christian realization of working on the temporal as a real consecration of the world to God in virtue of the command given to man by God in the act of creation.

74. Riesman, D., and others. *The Lonely Crowd*. Garden City, New York: Doubleday Anchor, 1953.

Once again, a popular sociology of modern times to gain an insight into the mentality and workings of modern man.

75. Russell, Bertrand. *The Impact of Science on Society*. New York: Columbia University Press, 1951.

Russell, of course, is a nonbeliever and as such sees science destroying the images of God and gods in an integration and ordering of man's knowledge by science. Interesting from the point of view of a nonbelieving philosopher.

76. Sagranyes de Franch, R., and others. *Foi et Technique*. XIII° Assemblee Pleniere de Pax Romana. Paris: Librarie Plon, 1959.

A series of various essays dedicated to the problems and directions of modern technology and society. Particularly interesting is the first article of Fr. Dondyne where he discusses the advantages and promises of technology for the Christian.

77. Scheler, Max. *Le Sens de La Sufrance*. Paris, 1946.

Keen psychological insights into the Christian and redemptive values of man's sufferings as a reparation for sin, as a sign of fraternal charity, and as redemptive of the whole cosmos.

78. Schollgen, W. *Christliche Soziologie als theologische Diszipliñ*. Die Neue Ordnung, 1947.

Once again an attempt to see the fundamental Christian reality at the base of a sound sociology. The author claims that the Christian possesses an optimistic view on the totality of social relation in and through the Mystical Body of Christ.

79. Schroedinger, E. *The Social Message of the New Testament*. Milwaukee: Bruce, 1937.

Attempts to show from the gospel texts of the New Testament a concrete Christian conception of the social order and the Christian's engagement in it.

80. Shuster, George, and others. *Catholicism in America*. New York: Harcourt, Brace and Co., 1954.

Various essays by Catholics and non-Catholics alike with reference to the problems of Christians in America. Problems with relation to tolerance, Church, State relations, culture, politics, etc., are all competently discussed.

81. Singer, C., and Holmyard, F. J. *History of Technology*. Oxford: Clarendon Press, 1954–1958. 5 vols.

About the most comprehensive work in the field, covering the entire field of technology from the earliest times to the present. Without a doubt, an absolutely necessary work in discussing the relationship between technology and Christianity.

82. Sorokin, P. *The Crisis of Our Age.* New York: E. P. Dutton & Co., 1941.

83. ———— *Social and Cultural Dynamics.* New York: American Book Co., 1937–1941.

One of the most eminent sociologists of our day discusses the problems of twentieth-century society. The last-cited work is particularly important work for getting a comprehensive view of the sociological problems of the United States.

84. Spicer, E. H., ed. *Human Problems in Technological Change.* New York: Russell Sage Foundation, 1952.

An attempt by the author to pose and then give some practical solutions to some of the more difficult of the problems posed by modern technology (advertisements, automation, etc.).

85. Thils, Gustav. *Christian Attitudes.* Chicago: Scepter Press, 1959.

86. ———— *Mission du Clergé et du Laicat.* Tournai: Desclée de Brouwer, 1945.

87. ———— *Orientations de la Théologie.* Louvain. Ed. Ceuterick, 1958.

88. ———— *Théologie des Realités Terrestres.* Bruges: Desclée de Brouwer, 1946–1948. 2 vols.

89. ———— *Théologie et Realité Sociale.* Tournai: Casterman, 1952.

Fr. Thils has probably done more in this field of Christian interpretation of the temporal order than any other single man on the continent. His books form a scriptural as well as theological basis for reflection on this particular problem. His books cover a diversity of subjects on this matter from sociology and the lay apostolate to an analysis of the two trends of Christian thinking in this matter.

90. Toynbee, A. J. *A Study of History.* London: Oxford University Press, 1934–1954. 10 vols.

91. ———— *A Study of History.* Abridgment by D. C. Somervell. New York: Oxford University Press, 1947–1957. 2 vols.

Toynbee remain one of the greatest living historians and as such deserves a respectful hearing. His controversial history is divided into stages in which he attempts to give a philosophical interpretation. Controversial but not to be neglected.

92. Vialatoux, J. *Signification Humaine du Travail.* Paris: ed. Oeuvr, 1953.

An attempt by the author to bring out the truly human aspects of various types of work and labor singly as a human and humane activity. He castigates certain forms of automation and attempts to give various solutions to the problem.

93. Ward, Barbara. *Five Ideas that Change the World*. New York: W. W. Norton & Co., 1959.

This Catholic author claims that these five ideas are essential for understanding the world of tomorrow. If her claim be true, then Christians must certainly take them into consideration in their relation in the world.

PART II

THEOLOGY OF THE LAY APOSTOLATE:
THE NEW CLASS

INTRODUCTION

So MUCH has been written on the theology of the layman in the Church during the past fifty years that bibliographies have been devoted to this subject alone.[1] It is not surprising, then, that this vast ecclesiological ferment has given birth to two worldwide congresses for the lay apostolate held at Rome in 1951 and 1957.[2] Pronouncements on this subject by Holy Fathers from Leo XIII to John XXIII have been so frequent that recently a complete volume was consecrated to this subject.[3]

All this thought and activity have been the result, at least indirectly, of the vast social and cultural changes of the past one hundred and fifty years. If it is erroneous to say that it is only in our day that the layman has "come of age,"[4] it is certainly true to say that it is only within the past century that the need for thought on the function of the layman in the Church has been felt in theological circles. There are many reasons for this, but the principal one has been the alienation of the modern world in most of its institutions from the Church's influence. Because of this alienation, the evangelical message of the Church can no longer be made known to the world by structures of a bygone era.[5] A new age is upon us for good or for evil; the structures and means of witness and evangelization have had to undergo some radical changes. Be-

---

[1] Cf. Bibliographical Note to this section, pp. 97–114.

[2] See the texts, reassembled by the permanent Committee for International Congresses of the Lay Apostolate. *Laymen in the Church: Texts* (Rome, 1958), 3 vols., and other publications by this standing committee.

[3] *Assembled Papal Texts on the Lay Apostolate* (Boston, 1960), published by St. Paul editions.

[4] Talk of His Holiness, Pius XII, to the Second International Congress for the Lay Apostolate: *Laymen in the Church*, I (Rome, 1958), pp. 13–34.

[5] D. J. Thorman, *The Emerging Layman* (New York, 1962), pp. 59–74.

cause of such a kaleidoscopic change, theologians have turned
their thoughts to the layman, a reality which has been always
present in the ecclesial body but which has not as yet been
fully investigated. The riches of a theology of the layman have
hardly been explored, but already we can see the great potentialities of this thought for the life of the Church.

The present position of the layman, then, is dictated by a
new functional need in the Church, a need to bring Christ
to a world which had lost Him. In many ways, a whole new
world has been constructed outside the Church and her influence and, in some cases, in spite of her protestations. In
the words of Cardinal Suhard: "Who is going to provide the
inspiration of this common civilization arising everywhere and
of itself, in a world hitherto divided — for this sudden unity
which has emerged more quickly than we realized — for a worldwide humanism for which we were unprepared? Who will make
the synthesis of the new universe? What will be its principle
and its inspiration?"[6] Will it be Communism, secularism,
agnosticism, or will it be Christ?

Encouraged by the sovereign pontiffs, theologians responded
that it must be Christ and that there was only one logical group
of Christians who could possibly do this — those actually engaged in the diverse functions of the modern world: in fac-
tories, families, colleges and universities, in the arts and professions, in the business world and industry. They were to be
Christ; by token of their baptism and confirmation their actions, in a true sense, were the very actions of Christ. As Pius
XII has stated: "Essentially, the 'Consecratio Mundi' is the
work of laymen themselves, of those who are intimately involved
in economic and social life, and who take part in government
and legislation. By the same token, Catholic cells among factory workers and among all laboring classes for the purpose of
bringing back to the Church those who are separated from it
can only be established by the workers themselves."[7]

---

[6] *The Church Today* (Chicago, 1953), p. 95.
[7] *Acta Apostolicae Sedis*, 49 (1957), 92.

The following chapters are an attempt to synthesize the findings of theologians on the subject of the lay apostolate. They do not pretend to be complete; they simply cover some of the areas already developed by theologians. This section will be divided into two parts. The first will deal with general dogmatic findings; the second with the possibility — to our mind, already certain — of a Christian humanism for the **layman.**

CHAPTER V

DOGMATIC CONSIDERATIONS

Vocabulary and Background

RECENT studies have clearly shown the biblical character of the word "layman." It is found in the Greek translation of the Hebrew Bible and signifies a holy people especially chosen by God as opposed to the pagans, the *ethnē*. The Israelites were the chosen people of God — the *laos* — who traveled through the desert, led and fed by God Himself. The decision to choose Israel was a free choice of God in which the Israelites could take no credit. It was simply God's mercy which descended on this particular people. When the writers responsible for the Septuagint aimed at expressing this unique character of Israel, they adopted the Greek word *laos*, giving it a sacred meaning. Israel was thus a nation set apart from all other nations, and in consequence of this choice by God it became sacred in character. In order to insure this sacred character, God gave Israel diverse privileges which were to help keep the sacredness of her vocation until the time of fulfillment in Christ: her worship in the temple, the covenant, the law, Sacred Scripture.

Yet all of these gifts to Israel, including her vocation as God's own sacred people (*laos*), were only temporary measures which were fulfilled in the coming of Christ. All of Israel's privileges were by their nature temporary, directed as they were toward the coming of Christ.[1] Those who accepted Christ have now

[1] "For the end of the law was Christ, unto the justification of everyone who believes." Rom 10:4. Cf. L. Cerfaux, *The Church in the Theology of St. Paul* (New York, 1959), pp. 7–82.

become the true Israel, those truly called by God, the true people of God (*laos*) consecrated by the blood of the Lamb Himself.[2] There is no longer any distinction between Jew and Greek, man and woman, slave and free man, for all have become one man in Christ.[3] Through Christ, the new nation of Christians is the final realization of God's plan, originally formulated in Israel but now achieving the ideal, God's Israel, God's people in Christ.

This thought — that Christians are God's sacred people — is clear in St. Paul. It is no wonder, then, that Pius XII objected to the idea that only in our day has the layman been "emancipated."[4] On the plane of vocation, the Christian calling in Christ, all are on the same level, for all belong without exception to this one people of God. If this unique people of God has diverse structures, its fundamental vocation is the same. The basic vocation in Christianity is to be called by God to become a part of His holy people, to become a Christian in the heart of Christ's extension on earth, the Mystical Body of Christ which is the Church. This is not to say that there are not diverse functions in the Church. From the very beginning, the ministerial priesthood and hierarchial office were always distinguished from the rest of the faithful of the Church. Yet these functions remain on a more secondary level. While the ministerial priesthood and the hierarchy receive their commission and consecration from Christ Himself, their office is still a means and exists for the whole people of God and not vice versa. The priesthood exists for God's community, not God's community for the priesthood. The fundamental dignity of all God's people is that they are the *membra Christi*, the *plebs tua Sancta*, consecrated to God in baptism and confirmation.

The layman, however, feels a certain *malaise* before his newly acquired status and responsibilities. He is faced with two psychological difficulties: one comes from the stupendous task

---

[2] Gal 3:29; 4:6; 6:15–16.

[3] Gal 3:28; 1 Cor 12:13.

[4] *Acta Apostolicae Sedis*, 49 (1957), 92–93; see English copy of this talk in *Laymen in the Church*, I (Rome, 1958), pp. 13–34.

which is before him in the modern world; the other comes from the fact that no former tradition exists which lays down a specific role and function for the layman regarding the world.

The present position of the layman becomes clear when looked at historically. Following the era of persecution in the postapostolic age came the time of the Church's influence in the body politic, culminating in the Middle Ages. Matters both sacred and profane were performed by the clergy, who alone could safeguard the whole political and religious traditions of the West in the wake of the barbarian invasions. Political thought was in its early stages, and the conflicts of Church and State from Pope St. Gregory VII to Boniface II only accentuated the difficulties in this regard. Even the liturgy became more and more a clerical function with the laity present as pious spectators. The culmination of this trend occurred when the liturgy came more and more to be looked on as an affair of the clergy, and in the Western Church there has been a parallel development in private devotions in the vernacular to offset the utter unintelligibility of the Latin liturgy.

From the early Middle Ages, ecclesiology has been characterized by a one-sidedness. Theologians and canonists emphasized clerical and pontifical authority rather than a total ecclesiology in which the interior and exterior aspects of the Church in all of its ramifications could be developed.

Jean Leclercq and George de la Garde have shown the beginning, and the resultant teaching, of ecclesiology to the present. Without entering into the gross exaggerations, condemned by Pius XII in his encyclical *Humani Generis*, we can truthfully say in the words of Yves Congar that ecclesiology from the thirteenth century on was built like the second Temple of the Jews, sword in hand.[5] The sword was pointed toward the encroachments on the Church by the State and her consequent struggle for freedom and independence. The struggle was started as far back as Gregory VII with the problem of lay investiture.

---

[5] Y. Congar, "La Pensée du Moehler et l'Ecclésiologie Orthodoxe," *Irénikon*, 12 (1935), 324.

The result during the later scholastic period was that the Church was conceived essentially as a juridical *societas* with its own rights, in opposition to, or rather in contrast with, the *societas civilis*. For the first time in history a religious body, in this case the Church, began to formulate this separation and independence vis-à-vis the secular power. Certainly, these notions were already apparent as far back as St. Ambrose and St. Augustine as well as in the famous "*duo sunt*" formula of Pope Gelasius in 494. The ultimate formulation of this concept, however, was left to the medieval canonists, during the struggles between Church and State throughout the Middle Ages. Thus began the separation of ecclesiology from the other aspects of theology, and its tone became apologetic and defensive in the face of secular and civil encroachments.[6] In later centuries arose the added difficulties of Conciliarism and the exaggerated elements of the "spiritual Church" of Ockham, Wycliffe, and Huss in opposition to the external and hierarchial element in the Church. These difficulties in turn led to a further emphasis in ecclesiology on the external elements of the Church. The proof of this excessive emphasis on the external aspects of the Church, due to both heresies and Conciliarism, is found in the work of one of the greatest ecclesiologists of the fifteenth century, Turrecremata and his famous *Summa de ecclesia*. The *Summa* is divided into five sections: (1) the Universal Church; (2) the Roman Church; (3) the Primacy of the Roman Pontiff; (4) Ecumenical Councils; (5) Schismatics and Heretics. The interior and spiritual element of the Church is not considered. The result, then, of this whole movement was an excessive emphasis on the hierarchial and external aspects of the Church. Even the titles of these first treatises *De ecclesia* betray their one-sided emphasis.

The earlier errors of Huss and Wycliffe, coupled with a pressing need for reform of the Church *in capite et in membris*,

---

[6] It is noteworthy to observe that St. Thomas did not treat the Church outside of the total context of its relationship to the other Christian mysteries in his *Summa Theologiae, Pars Secunda*.

led to the revolt of the sixteenth century. Once again for the Reformers, the external structure of the Church was relegated not only to the secondary and nonessential but to sinfulness itself. The ecclesiological elaborations since this period have been dominated by polemics between the Church and the Reform. Abundant evidence of this can be found in such eminent ecclesiologists as Stapleton (1598) and Bellarmine (1621). After this period, ecclesiology takes on a strictly apologetical point of view in defense of the hierarchy, clergy, sacraments, etc. — in short, the visible aspect of the Church. It became, in the words of Congar, a true "hierarchiology"[7] instead of a total ecclesiology.

Starting in this same period, we have further errors which only served to harden the above tendency: Gallicanism, Jansenism, Febronianism, Josephism, and finally, in Germany, Episcopalianism. All these errors had in common the denial of the Church in one or other element of her hierarchial structure or teaching authority. These could be combated only by emphasis on the Church as an independent society, with a divinely constituted hierarchy and teaching authority. Against all these errors and encroachments, ecclesiologists tended to define the Church not only as a spiritual institution but also as a society, properly speaking, which was visible, institutionally unequal and hierarchial, independent, and having its own spiritual finality, with the authority on earth to judge in a visible and judicial way. The authority of the bishops, and above all that of the Sovereign Pontiff, Vicar of Jesus Christ, is heavily emphasized throughout this period.

From this short analysis, it is easy to see why, theologically and ecclesiologically, there has been little thought given to the position of the layman in the Church.

During the past hundred and fifty years, however, a radical transformation of the political-social structure of the Western world has occurred, and the Church can no longer exert any

---

[7] Y. Congar, "Affirmation de l'autorité," l'Ecclésiologie au XIXe Siècle (Paris, 1961), p. 113.

direct influence on society. It has become more and more clear
that if she is still to exert her salvific influence in society, it
must be through the intermediary of her officially consecrated
laymen. In the words of St. Thomas they are consecrated *quasi
ex officio*, to bear witness in the world, to bring Christ into the
structures of society in word and work.[8]

If this modern revolution of society has caused much suffering to the Church, it has also had as a beneficial result the
fact that the function of the layman in the Church has become
ever more clear and formulated. *Bonum ex malo*. Indeed, one
may add, it would seem that the very notion of the Church
as the society and community of salvation has become ever
more clear in the eyes of believers and unbelievers alike. Her
spiritual mission is unencumbered by secular disputes and
animosities which came to her from a too deep immersion into
the body politic and people temporal. This, of course, is not
to say that her mission to men in the city of man has ended;
it simply means that this mission is now conducted by those
of her members whose proper existence is the temporal order.
The Church's temporal and social mission is always indirect.
Her competent authority expounds the principles of justice and
charity. These, however, must be adapted to the thousand temporal contingencies at hand, and this adaptation can be properly
performed only by those engaged in that existence: laymen. In
this way, both her spiritual mission and her intervention in
society are justly guaranteed. This link between the Church
and the modern world, which is the layman, seems to be the
most perfect way of describing his function within the Church.
To quote the words of Pius XII:

> Before all else the Church progressed in depth, only thereafter
> in extent. In the first place, she seeks man himself, using all her
> endeavors to form and fashion him, to perfect God's likeness in
> him. She does her work in each one's heart, but affects the whole
> of life and every individual activity. In men thus formed, the
> Church provides a firm foundation of human society.

---

[8] *S.T.*, III, q. 72, a. 2.

And now what follows for the Church? Today, more than ever, she must believe her mission; more energetically than ever she must repulse that narrow and false conception of her spirituality and inward life which would confine her, blind and dumb, to the recesses of the sanctuary. The Church cannot shut herself up, inactive, in the privacy of her churches and thus neglect the mission entrusted to her by Divine Providence, the mission to form man in his fullness and so ceaselessly to collaborate in building the solid basis of society. This mission is of her essence. Looking at her from this standpoint, it can be said that the Church is the society of those who, under the supernatural influence of grace, in the perfection of their personal dignity as sons of God and in the harmonious development of every human bent and energy, build up the mighty framework of the community of men.

From this aspect the faithful, more precisely the laity, are in the front line of the Church's life; through them, the Church is the vital principle of human society. Consequently, they particularly must have an ever more clear consciousness, not only of belonging to the Church, but of being the Church. . . .[9]

Function of Laymen in the Church

There is little doubt among most theologians that the proper role of laymen in the Church, as noted previously, is to be the official mediators between the world and the Church.[10] This mediation entails two distinct notions: the first is that laymen are truly consecrated for this task; the second, that the temporary domain as such has a true meaning for the Christian.

Adult Christianity. The term "adult" is not so strange as it may appear. "For a world which is growing to adulthood, we have to build up an adult Christianity."[11] For this tremendous task, Christians must and can find the renovating

---

[9] Address to Cardinals, February 20, 1946.

[10] G. Philips, *The Role of the Laity in the Church* (Chicago, 1956), p. 204; G. Thils, *Théologie des Realités Terrestres,* I (Paris, 1949), pp. 62–80; W. Ong, *American Catholic Crossroads* (New York, 1959), pp. 67–159; Pierre de Chardin, *The Divine Milieu* (New York, 1960), pp. 30–65; J. Maritain, *True Humanism* (New York, 1954), pp. 40–65; A. Lambert, "Malaise de la Conscience Chrétienne devant les tâches Temporelles," *Révue Nouvelle,* 6 (1954), 592–602.

[11] Address of Bishop M. Larrain, in *Laymen in the Church,* I (Rome, 1958), p. 155.

principle in a proper understanding of their own consecration to Christ in the sacraments of baptism and confirmation.

The sacrament of confirmation is the sacrament of spiritual adulthood, officially deputizing a man to bear witness both in word and deed for Christ in the world. St. Thomas says that this function of witness is official, *quasi ex officio.*[12] Baptism, explains St. Thomas, is a sacrament which sanctifies the Christian in his individual person; he receives this sacrament as a personal sanctification and consecration in and to Christ.[13] On the other hand, while given to the baptized, confirmation is conferred so that the Christian might radiate his spiritual influence to others. While all the sacraments have a social function, confirmation alone is specifically given for the exterior apostolate of witness.

Each of the sacraments of baptism, confirmation, and holy orders imprints a character on the soul. This character permits us to participate in the power of Christ to worship. Confirmation, moreover, makes us capable of the profession of faith in an official capacity because it unites us with the God-man insofar as He was essentially the supreme witness of God. The confirmed is the authentic instrument and voice of Christ in the world, *quasi ex officio*. This profession of faith, in consequence, is a true act of worship, a continuous praise of God in and through this witness of Christ in whatever vocation the confirmed chooses to follow. This witness, then, is an act of cult, which is for the confirmed a continuous source of grace and sanctification in the very act of witness in the world. It is the duty of the confirmed person, and of him alone, to confess his faith before the enemies of Christian worship. And his confession has a real value that is at once sacred and objective, a value which the confession of the simply baptized does not have.

---

[12] *S.T.*, III, 9, 72, a. 5, ad 2.

[13] *Ibid.*, q. 66, a. 1, in *Corpore*. "In this Sacrament, the fullness of the Holy Spirit is given for the spiritual strength which belongs to the perfect age. But when a man comes to perfect age, he then begins to benefit others through his actions; whereas previously he lived solely for himself, as it were" (III, q. 72, a. 2, in *Corpore*).

The sacrament of confirmation can almost be called the sacrament of the lay apostle. The strength (*dynamis*) of the Holy Spirit is given specifically for this witness of Christ to the external world. In the ancient Church, bearing witness went as far as martyrdom, which means, etymologically, "to bear witness." Those who are confirmed are henceforth responsible for the Christian truth and the Church of Christ. The witness of their confirmation is authentic because it bears the virtue (strength) of the Holy Spirit Himself and also because it is embedded in the testimony of the Church through its sacramental character.[14]

It is easy to see how this notion gives the whole of the lay apostolate its *raison d'être*. The duty of witness is not exclusively that of the hierarchy but of the whole of the people of God who have been so consecrated by baptism and, above all, by confirmation. The witness of the lay apostle will have an authentic value before the whole world. It is precisely here that the lay apostle is the essential link between the Church and the world which does not know Christ. Consecrated in confirmation, the lay Christian has the duty and obligation of becoming and representing Christ to the world into which he is officially sent.[15]

The Layman and the Temporal. The word "world" leads us to the problem of the Christian signification of terrestrial activities. We have seen that Catholic authors have stressed the bond of relationship between the layman and the temporal world. The lay Christian is officially and authentically sent into the world by the Church to bear witness for Christ. Can we, however, go deeper into this relationship between the Christian and the world? In this area there seems to be a sharp difference of opinion among theologians. All authors are agreed

---

[14] D. M. Stanley, "The New Testament Doctrine of Baptism," in *Theological Studies*, 17 (1957), 169–215; J. Crehan, "Ten Years' Work on Baptism and Confirmation," *Theological Studies*, 16 (1956), 494–515; P. T. Camelot, "Toward a Theology of Confirmation," *Theology Digest*, 7 (1959), 67–71.

[15] See letter of Pius XI to the Cardinal of Lisbon, November 10, 1933: "Confirmatione nempe Jesu Christi milites efficimur; atque militi cuique non tam pro suo quam pro ceterorum bono elaborandum. . . ."

that the temporal must occupy an essential dimension in the vocation of laymen. It must not be reduced simply to a means to an end, salvation, but must somehow be truly and really transformed by his activity. We have already attempted to give a Christian interpretation of diverse temporal activities, and there is no need to return to it here. We can take it for granted that such a thing as Christian humanism exists and is generally accepted among Catholic theologians. Although there remain many practical difficulties as to its practical impregnation into society, the validity of a Christian humanism is generally accepted today.

We have already mentioned the fact that the layman, in the function of his royal, kingly, and prophetical office, received in the sacraments of baptism and confirmation, is the extension of Christ and the Church in the modern secularistic and materialistic world. There is little doubt that in this regard the message of the Church to society, her mission to the temporal city of men, will remain largely unheard unless it be through her officially designated apostles, the laymen.

Sent into the world of temporal realities, laymen become a sign to the world of unbelieving men. Christ can no longer be present to the world in any physical way as He was in Palestine some 2000 years ago. He must do this through those who are His extension in space and time, the laymen in the Church. But here we must have a distinction: Christ was, above all, the supreme sign of God; by contemplating religiously the words and works of Christ, men have to come to some conclusion concerning His mission. The Gospel of St. John never calls the works of Christ miracles; by always calling them *semeia* (signs), the sacred author wished to put the accent on the supernatural aspect of the reality and not simply on its extraordinary character. In these signs we see a revealing element of the presence and personal action of God in Christ. An attitude begins to take shape within a person according to the way he reacts to this sign which he has encountered. The dramatic character of the signs is portrayed for us throughout the Gospel of St. John. They create a psychological attitude in the one who contemplates them; they create the option between death and life, faith or unbelief.[16]

In a very similar way, the Christian as Christ's representative by virtue of his baptism and confirmation becomes the faithful witness or sign of Christ to an unbelieving world. Since Christ can no longer be physically present to express this sign, this must now come about by the lay Christian in the world. Lay Christians must further the kingdom of heaven and this sign of Christ in all temporal domains. One thinks of the domain of art and culture where a false image of man, who was created in the image of God, is so frequent. One thinks of the sign of Christian heroism of an Adenauer, a De Gaulle, a De Gasparri in the field of politics; one thinks of the heroic sign portrayed in those Catholic organizations which take part in the UN, strengthening it, reminding it of its special duties to man. Speaking to the new minister of El Salvador, Pius XII urged the smaller nations and Catholic organizations not "to renounce the use" of the forum of the UN but to employ it "to prod the conscience of the world."[17] One thinks of the sign of the truly Christian home or of a parish whose people love one another deeply. Even so common a thing as an expression of solicitude, sympathy, and warmhearted friendliness by a lay Christian testifies as a sign of Christ's charity to the world. All this, it might be added, is a definite act of worship on the part of the confirmed lay Christian. This testimony, this witness of Christ's love for the world, is a continuous and dynamic function of the character of the sacrament of confirmation. This character, as we have already said, makes us participate in the power of the Lord to worship.

We have seen that the sacramental character of baptism renders the Christian similar to Christ by making him capable of truly offering the Holy Sacrifice of the Mass in and through

---

[16] See Jn 3:36; 5:24; 11:25; 13:31.
[17] Cited in "Pius XII and the UN," by Msgr. H. C. Koenig in Catholic Mind, 52 (1954), 143–148.

the priest. It has, therefore, a sacrificial character and assimilation. Now all worship involves a deep and personal profession of faith in Christ. This profession of faith in baptism makes us capable of God's operation of superior praise in the Holy Sacrifice because it unites and assimilates us to the God-man. In confirmation, we are assimilated to Christ and are rendered more like Him in His witness to the presence and truth of God. For just as the Christian is the extension of Christ in the world, he is also, by virtue of the sacrament of confirmation, as far as he reproduces the prophetical office, Christ's witness in the world.[18] The profession of faith, the proclamation of the truth and holiness of Christianity which come from a confirmed person in the world, is agreeable to God; it is authentic and certain because its basic value of profession comes from the Incarnate Word, of whom the confirmed person is at this moment and in this place, as it were, the instrument and the temporal voice. These signs of charity, proposed by the confirmed to the world for its wonderment, are truly and authentically acts of true worship and are agreeable to God because, by the sacramental seal, the confirmed has become identified and assimilated to the office of the witnessing and prophetical Christ. His actions so posed, in both the natural and supernatural spheres, are both signs to the unbelieving and believing world and, above all, acts of worship agreeable to God. In this sense, the notion of the priesthood of the faithful both in its sacrificial and witnessing aspects becomes clearly well founded in dogmatic theology. "All Christians, by virtue of their baptism, have received the capacity to make an offering in Christ and with Christ."[19] The term "priesthood of the faithful" must be viewed both as sacrifice and witness. Lay people truly offer the Holy Sacrifice in an authentic way by and through the ministerial priesthood; but, as Msgr. Cerfaux has noted so well, the term *Regale Sacerdotum* was used principally by Christian

---

[18] See the illuminating chapter "The Laity and the Church's Prophetical Function" in Y. Congar's book: *Lay People in the Church*, pp. 258–308.

[19] E. J. DeSmedt, *The Priesthood of the Faithful* (New York, 1962), p. 21.

tradition to designate the example and spiritual witness of Christians before the gentiles and pagans. "It is the whole Christian community, united with the Apostles and prophets, as in one complete organism, which renders a spiritual cult to God."[20]

The witness of Christians to the world is imperative in our day. There is no need to cite the moral and spiritual poverty of the so-called culture of the "Judeo-Christian" West. In a growing majority of nations, even in the West, the state and most of its institutions are, for all practical purposes, officially neutral toward religion. Inclusive in this are almost all of the universities and other institutions of learning. As Father Norris Clarke, citing two Presbyterian theologians, remarks:

> The well-adjusted mid-20th century man, beautifully trained to a high level of mass consumption . . . is extremely difficult to describe as one who finds his ultimate concern in death, let alone God. . . . He is anxious, disquieted, often desperate, but his anxieties seem orientated around his professional and social status, his sexual relations and the dislocating of a revolutionary world. . . . He no longer lives in a Hebrew-Christian era, and what is more, he no longer wants to. . . . It is not just . . . Christian assumptions which are being questioned by the modern secular mood, but all religions, and even all attempts to give meaning to reality as a whole and man's destiny in it.[21]

We need not carry the investigation any further. Without being the Cassandra of doom, we can safely say that the witness of laymen to the world is needed today more than at any other time in the world's history. As Fr. Rahner says, in stating the condition proper to the laity, the decisive factor is that their Christian function is determined by their situation in the world,[22] that is, by their natural commitment to the work of the world which they do not give up in order to serve God's

---

[20] L. Cerfaux, "Regale Sacerdotium," *Receuil L. Cerfaux*, II (Gembloux, 1954), p. 303.

[21] Norris Clarke, S.J., "Is the West 'God's Civilization'?" *America* 106 (March 31, 1962), p. 854.

[22] "l'Apostolat des laics," *Nou. Rév. Théo.*, 78 (1956), 3–32; cf. also Y. Congar, *Laity, Church, World* (Baltimore, 1961), pp. 60–72.

kingdom. They must become sanctified, not in spite of it, but precisely in it and through it. Yet we must add immediately that the lay person is characterized as Christian in the world precisely through and by the priestly, kingly, and prophetical functions conferred on him by baptism and confirmation. He is now a member of the Mystical Body of Christ to keep the word and officially confess it before men by impregnating all temporal duties and professions with the spirit of Christ. Thus will he become Christ's sign, that he may profess and confess the faith in the world and before men's eyes.

The action of the layman in the world will have both a fundamental unity and a distinction. The unity will come from the fact that God and Christ have one intention, one will with regard to all creation (inclusive of the temporal). The idea of Christ will be the driving force of every authentic Christian humanism and work in the world. To deny this is tantamount to saying that God has no interest in the temporal realities of man. Pauline theology states clearly that all is created for and through Christ, both as efficient and final cause. Yet we must clearly distinguish between the natural and the supernatural. While both are united in the intention of the Creator and in the view of Christian faith, still this same faith does not absorb all into a generic unity. There is a unity of intention without any confusion of the two realities. Precisely at this juncture we must locate the position of the layman in a complete ecclesiology. This intention will be to further the kingdom of Christ by infusing Christian attitudes into the temporal domain; this is so because no human intention (politics, government, education, trade agreements, family life, legislation, etc.) is ever devoid of either spiritual or material structures. The Christian idea (or if Christians fail, materialistic, pragmatic, etc., idea) becomes incarnate in these diverse human words and actions. All of man's spiritual projects develop in the measure that they become the heart of the temporal work. These spiritual intentions become incarnate in man's temporal activities and thus the external project is nothing but the outward extension of this one spiritual intention. Therefore, all activities of the Christian remain one in their supernatural and Christian intention. The human and temporal projections have their source in this one intention of faith which sees, in a sense, all with God's eyes. This one intention makes the Christian correspond to God's intention in faith. The human and temporal realities, however, remain human and temporal, but their inner structures, their intentions, their inner spiritual driving force have become Christian through and by the activity of Christian laymen in the world.

God wills this unity of faith without confusion of domains in all of men's dimensions. The mistake of ancient Israel and even of the latter Middle Ages was to put all human achievements and activities at the direct service of the supernatural end. The Renaissance emancipated human activity from the exclusive service of the supernatural end. This "emancipation" had both a good and a bad effect. The bad effect is abundantly clear in the separation of human activity and its intention from the faith; this has come to be known in our day as secularism. The good result was that human activity achieved its own dignity as willed by the Creator. Yet this activity must receive its basic unity in God's intention. Only with the light of faith can the Catholic layman safeguard the ultimate dignity of human endeavor. Faith alone will give him the proper equilibrium between the two. By refusing faith in the intention of the Creator, there is real danger that modern civilization will close in upon itself in a rationalism and temporal and terrestrial messianism. This is exactly what has happened in Marxism and this is exactly what is happening in Western culture.[23] It has been said, with some truth, that Communism is the logic of Christian messianism turned completely temporal and terrestrial. The layman is the only hope for the world of today — the layman with Christian faith and intention. He has the very difficult and awesome task of keeping both

[23] B. Ward, *The Rich Nations and the Poor Nations* (New York, 1962), pp. 21–25.

supernatural and natural domains intact while at the same time procuring for the temporal, in which he is professionally engaged, the radical unity given him by his faith. Laymen must, therefore, be concerned with advancing true progress in various sectors of society since the Gospel has little chance of success in an environment where truly human values are threatened. Animated with the intentions of Christ, they must transform and engage fully the temporal activities of the world. Christians must not be accused of a truncated humanism whereby they separate, in a nonunitive way, the human from the divine. The intention of the believer must unite both Christ's intention to the human endeavor without confusing the two. The layman is not a "layman" and a "Christian" juxtaposed. One cannot put the accent more on one than the other. He is totally human and totally changed and elevated by Christ. He must work to promote faith and civilization by uniting them without confusing them. His human abilities remain human, and he must perfect them to promote civilization as Christ wills it; he must furthermore learn to see God's reflection in all that he does. The great movement, for example, to fill the leisure time produced by our technological age by raising the level of the community to the beauties of God's creation by music, drama, cultural TV programs and movies, books, and singing is certainly a humanizing influence which corresponds to the deep wishes of Christ. Technology, for example, with all its drawbacks, has produced a tremendous humanizing influence which cannot be denied: men have been freed from the slavery of the earth, from dangers of famine, from the dehumanizing forces of nature. This has certainly been in the intention of the Creator, and the layman must learn to see God in and through that work. These activities, authors point out, serve to show the great dignity of the layman and of his work in the world.

Does the temporal have a Christian sense or not? Does it reflect the intentions of Christ or not? If we answer in the negative, then we relegate the layman to a pure "receiver" of

Church doctrine and the sacraments without any real active apostolate of their own. In that case, K. Rahner is correct in saying that laymen can be called apostles in the full sense only on condition of abandoning their lay state and passing, to the degree that they have an apostolate to apply Christian principles to the secular domain, to the ranks of the clergy.[24] If the temporal has a real Christian meaning — to be informed by lay Christians with Christ's intentions, to be developed to the fullest degree as God's reflection of Himself — then the layman has found his proper apostolate and vocation in the Church, received from Christ in the very fact of his baptism and confirmation.

[24] Art. cit., pp. 3–6.

CHAPTER VI

LAY SPIRITUALITY AND CHRISTIAN HUMANISM

THE notion of diverse forms of spirituality — in the sense of
varied means of applying the eternal Christian truths to one's
life — has been well developed in theological circles.[1] Every
Christian, regardless of his category as priest, religious, or layman, is a full citizen in the Church. In this sense there can
be no "special class" of privileged souls in the bosom of the
Church. The sacraments of baptism and confirmation have
made all citizens equal in the Church. Incorporated into Christ
by the consecration which is baptism, and further consecrated
and strengthened in that faith by confirmation so that he may
be Christ's witness to the world, the Christian has within himself the seeds of grace that will radically determine his spiritual
life. While authors concede that diverse applications of Christian spirituality are needed, v.g., to the married, religious,
sacerdotal life, these orientations must always remain rooted in
divine bonds making the Christian truly and existentially another Christ, a *membrum Christi* in the Mystical Body of
Christ. Baptism will always remain at the origin of all spiritual-
ities. Perhaps it would be better to speak of the radical unity of
Christian spirituality in view of its unique source — the grace
of Christ given in baptism. As we have already pointed out,

---

[1] J. Folliet, *World Catholicism Today* (Westminster, Md., 1961), pp. 130–
169; G. Philips, *The Role of the Layman in the Church* (Chicago, 1956), pp.
147–167; J. M. Perrin, *Christian Perfection and Married Life* (Westminster,
Md., 1958); G. Thils, *Christian Holiness* (Tielt, 1961), pp. 2–44; D. Dohen,
"Problems of the Lay Christian," in *Cross and Crown*, 9 (1957), 400–407.

but in another context, the sacrament of baptism conforms us to Christ in an ontological, that is, real way. This radical root and "germ" of divine life, which is our configuration to Christ, must continue to grow into the full image of Christ which we are to reproduce in our lives.[2] In other words, the baptismal character has marked us with the imprint of the image of Christ which must continuously develop if we are to reach Christian and spiritual maturity.[3] The imitation of Christ, the continuous effort to bring all our actions, thoughts, and hopes into conformity with what we are — sons of God in Christ — is the supreme law of Christianity. In this sense, there can be no "privileged class," for all in the Church have been incorporated into her and into Christ and, consequently, can never escape this basic and essential obligation. The early Fathers of the Church saw this most clearly. St. Ignatius of Antioch, writing to the Christians of Philadelphia, said: "Be imitators of Jesus Christ as He is of His Father."[4] Origen compared this daily imitation of Christ by the Christian to a real, though bloodless, martyrdom and this, he claimed, was the natural consequence of the Christian's baptism into Christ.[5] All ulterior consecrations and dedications to Christ which can be added to this fundamental engagement (v.g., sacerdotal or religious) will only come to accentuate and make more profound this baptismal consecration. What is first and foremost in Christian life is the fundamental and original *imitatio Christi* given to the Christian on the day of his

[2] Rom 8:28–29: "Now we know that in all things which are for their good, God works together with those who love him, who according to his purpose are called; for those whom he has foreknown he has also predestined to be conformed to the image of his Son, so that this Son should be the first-born among many brothers."

[3] P. Riga, "Mortification, Penance, and Love," *Cross and Crown*, 13 (1961), 12–14.

[4] See the many texts throughout all of his letters. *Ad Philad.* 7, 2; *Ad Ephe.* 10, 3; *Ad Rom.* 6, 3, where he says: "Permit me to be an imitator of the passion of my God."

[5] Origen, exorting his friends Ambrose and Protoctetus to martyrdom, recalls to them the demands of their baptism, *Exortatio ad Marty.* 12 (*P.G.* 11, 577).

baptism. In another profound sense, baptism is the gauge for the final coming of Christ when He will come in glory for His own. Baptism already anticipates the final coming of Christ in glory. The gospel narratives are very evident in the solemn address by the priest to the newly baptized: "Receive this lighted candle, and keep your baptism above reproach. Keep the commandments of God, so that when the Lord comes to His marriage feast, you may meet Him in the halls of Heaven with all His saints, and live with Him forever."[6]

This "sanctity," however, is a very complex reality. Upon clearer examination it implies two irreducible characteristics: the divine life living in the Christian and, in addition, his temporal vocation. The Christian is, in the words of St. Augustine, a citizen of two worlds in which he must take an active and real part. We have already discussed the reality of the change effected in the Christian by virtue of his baptism. This infusion of grace, of course, is absolutely essential to the reality of Christian life. Without it, Christianity is reduced to an impotent humanism. On the other hand, some stress this aspect of Christian life to such a degree that the temporal vocation and apostolate of the Christian to the world is left almost unnoticed. To do this is to reduce Christianity to a barren contemplation of God with no repercussions in the temporal order. The true Catholic notion of sanctity is to respect the complex character of these two fundamental realities while trying to find an equilibrium for both. In reading the New Testament, St. Paul or St. John, for example, one has the impression that the basic supernatural transformation of the Christian's life by grace ought necessarily to lead to a radical transformation of his action in the world and upon it. One recognizes the disciple of Christ by his external life, by his conduct and attitudes in the face of all reality and existence. His faith must communicate and inform his temporal activities. We must recognize that, on the one hand, Christianity has a

---

[6] Translation taken from *Collectio Rituum* (Milwaukee, 1955), p. 31 ff. which refers to Mt 25:1–12, 25.

value in itself quite independent of its repercussions in the temporal order, and, on the other hand, that it is absolutely necessary for one to be preoccupied with these repercussions if one does not wish Christianity to evaporate, to lose contact with the concrete world of human existence. These two aspects — the divine life and temporal vocation — seem so essential to Christianity that it is impossible to sever them in any way, relegating one to one distinct category of Christians, and the other to another. The fundamental desire on the part of every Christian must be to combine them in Catholic action. They must be wedded harmoniously both in the life of laymen and in the life of those who are consecrated more to meditation and prayer. This temporal vocation — the incarnation of Christian attitudes and ideas into temporal realities in all of their ramifications — is not simply desirable; it is absolutely necessary.[7] We might call these the two irreducible principles of all Christian spiritual life.[8]

This total dedication to Christ, which is a necessary corollary of baptismal consecration, has been sometimes obscured by a certain type of propaganda for the religious life. One sometimes hears it said that, if one wishes to give oneself entirely to Christ, one must become a priest or a religious. There is certainly an element of truth in this kind of statement correctly understood, but the fact remains that it has led and can still lead to some confusion for lay people.[9] Even the term "vocation" has been ambiguous in some religious literature. The radical vocation of all in the Church is life in God by, with, and through Christ. This vocation is universal in its scope and all-encompass-

---

[7] For more elaboration in this regard, see St. Francis De Sales, *Introduction to the Devout Life* (Garden City, N. Y., 1956), pp. 124–128; C. Pepler, *The Three Degrees* (London, 1957), pp. 27–50; *Complete Works of St. Theresa*, trans. E. A. Peers, II (New York, 1946), pp. 329–350; Dom Chautard, *The Soul of the Apostolate* (Gethsemani, Ky.: 1946). The combination of these two "dimensions" of Christian life is the whole theme of this last book; Y. De Montcheuil, *A Guide for Social Action* (Chicago, 1954), pp. 51–57.

[8] J. E. Haley, ed., *Apostolic Sanctity in the World. A Symposium on Total Dedication in the World and Secular Institutes* (Notre Dame, Ind., 1957), pp. 50–78; Ida Görres, *The Nature of Sanctity* (New York, 1954).

[9] D. Dohen, art. cit., *Cross and Crown*, 9 (1957), 400–407.

ing in its dimensions. The fundamental vocation is to be "another Christ," to reproduce His image in each individual Christian life. In other words, the gift of each Christian must be total. In this sense, there can be no differences between the religious and the layman. There is, however, a difference on a secondary level. The layman is to live totally for Christ, but his state of life *includes*, by necessity, earthly goods (family, temporal goods, autonomy), whereas the religious is to live totally for Christ but *exclusive* of earthly goods or their direct ownership. The further dignity of the religious comes from the example he gives the world of the superiority of supernatural goods over all others which, however, are good in themselves.[10] Perhaps in explaining the notion of poverty, it would be better to stress the positive element of using earthly goods according to God's will than to emphasize, as has been traditional, the negative theme of "giving things up." This, perhaps, would be more in conformity to the layman's function with regard to the whole of the temporal order. This, of course, presupposes a further analysis of the secondary forms of vocation in Christian life. Theologians here generally distinguish the "sacred" vocation from the "profane" vocation. The sacred vocations hold their preeminence in that they are directly related to the extension of God's kingdom on earth. They are completely identified with the work of the Church as such: worship, sanctification, prayer, etc. Yet even in the sphere of the "sacral," the layman has sometimes a very important and natural function to perform. As an example, Catholic young men and women confer the sacrament of matrimony on each other in the marriage contract. The spouses are the proper ministers of this sacrament, and as a result their entire life has a consecrated, sacral character. There are other properly sacred functions which are in the direct competence of laymen. The mother and father who train their little ones in the ways of God are performing the very ancient

---

[10] This is the general theme of many of the pastoral sermons of Pope St. Leo the Great, *Epist* 4, 7, 19, 25, 65, 99, 167. Cf. P. Battiffol, "Leon Ier," *DTC*, IV (Paris, 1917), cols. 219–222.

custom of the *traditio symboli*. In the early Church when most of the candidates for baptism were adults, the bishop, a few days before their baptism, would give them a copy of the "symbol of Faith" to be guarded and kept all the days of their life. Now that most of the baptized are babies, this function belongs properly to the mother and the father who officially, in the name of the Church, give their children the first rudiments of faith by their deeds and words. Under certain circumstances, moreover, the laity can be charged by the hierarchy to teach catechism officially and to this degree they enter into the sacred order. We have seen this frequently in recent times in the widespread use of lay catechists.

Yet, in general, the vocation of laymen will remain "profane"; that is, their actions are directly oriented toward earthly goods which they must attempt to imbue with Christian values and ideals. The first glory of this vocation is to transform the world of matter into a cultural milieu in which man can live in dignity as man, a prerequisite to his becoming a Son of God. We may take the work of a scientist as one example among many. Science, in general, attempts to disclose in some sense, however oblique, the hidden structures of the real. The scientist is charged with interpreting this body of nature in which God reveals Himself no less surely, though much less clearly, than in the Bible. What the scientist finds is what God Himself has put there — the intelligible structures which are the proper objects of man's God-given intellect.[11] The sublime vocation of the scientist is to reveal this God of Love through the miracles of His creation.[12] In this way, as we have already pointed out, man has a share in the dominion of God over all of creation. Did He not create the material and natural universe? One

---

[11] E. McMullin, "Science and the Catholic Tradition," *America*, 102 (1959), 346–349.

[12] For the merit of these different human endeavors done by those who do not believe in God, see St. Thomas, *Summa Theologiae* I–II, q. 109, a. 2, and II–II q. 23, a. 7, ad 1. They are what St. Thomas would have called imperfectly good, since morally human action, in order to be perfectly good, must be ordered toward man's last end. See Commentary on this section of the *Summa* by R. Mulard, *Somme Théologique* (Paris, 1948), pp. 251–255.

sometimes wonders about this when he hears some Christians speak of profane activities, say, of the scientist, comparing them unfavorably to formal ecclesiastical works.

We must also stress that the vocation in the temporal and profane orders can be — and for the true follower of Christ must be — redemptive; laymen alone, who are properly consecrated to the temporal and earthly, can assure the place of the inspirations of Christ and the dominion of the Spirit in the world. The whole of the temporal order must become, by the work of laymen, Christian, without becoming properly supernatural. Activities such as politics, government, trade, and family life must all reflect the intentions and orientations of Christ. This, of course, is the basic meaning of Christian humanism. In short, the laity need to become more and more convinced of this point of view. This view of their profane vocation is properly and truly Christian. This attitude does not try to deny the nonsupernatural character of the earthy work that is the layman's proper concern. Yet it does recognize the supernatural character of the layman himself and the vocation he has, as a *membrum Christi*, to bathe terrestrial realities with the light of the Gospel. The profane world cannot be considered as banal and unimportant for Christ because it is not supernatural. As a matter of fact, it is becoming more and more clear in our day of global revolution of all kinds that unless a society is first of all human, it has little chance of becoming Christian. From this follows the basic Christian meaning of every profession and trade. In the words of a great spiritual writer: "According to the Catholic concept, every participation in work in the world, every cultural activity is a vocation willed by God. Its exercise is a religious activity in the widest sense. Since human life is in its totality orientated toward God, all work is a service of God. For one who grasps this idea there can be no possible opposition between civilization and religion."[13] The lawmaker who attempts to make more humane laws for

[13] L. Malevez, "Philosophie Chrétienne du progrès," *Nou. Rév. Théo.*, 34 (1937), 377–385.

criminal punishment as well as the priest who distributes Communion to the sick are both performing Christian actions, even though not of the same order. The fact that the action of the priest has a greater dignity than that of the lawmaker does not in the least take away from the Christian dignity of the second. A solid spirituality for laymen must take these factors into account under pain of "putting lay people in a false situation by making them look for sanctity outside of their milieu."[14] Perhaps the layman's temporal engagement will have to be stressed more now than in the past, when certain types of literature attempted to make him a sort of half religious who must join third orders in order to participate fully in Christian life. This was, in a sense, the idea behind many of the accounts of the saints' lives written during the Middle Ages. These hagiographers described their saints in terms of legends in which, say, the prince did not become a saint because he ruled well or governed justly, but because he lived like a monk or established a religious order. One has the impression that there were few lay saints in past centuries who attained sanctity as lay people and still fewer lay married saints. Such organizations as the Christian Family Movement, the Young Christian Workers, diverse lay councils on civil liberties, study groups of lawyers and doctors are all happily remedying this situation and returning once again to what has always been the traditional and fundamental doctrine of the Church: one must not only sanctify oneself in one's state of life but must further extend one's Christianity to all of these diverse sectors of temporal life. More thought is needed, however, on the relationship of the temporal to Christian life. Since lay spirituality and its relation to the kingdom necessarily depend on this, more speculation by theologians is needed. Here a quotation from Pierre Teilhard de Chardin is pertinent: "God does not deflect our gaze prematurely from the work He Himself has given us, since He presents Himself to us as attainable through that very

---

[14] G. Philips, "l'Etat actuel de la pensée Théologique . . . ," *Eph. Theo. Lov.,* 35 (1959), 900.

work. . . . We ought to accustom ourselves to this basic truth until we are steeped in it. . . . He is waiting for us at every moment in our action, in our work of the moment. He is in some sort at the tip of my pen, my spade, my brush, my needle — of my heart and of my thought."[15]

Perhaps a special word ought to be said about the Christian spirituality of marriage.[16] It is said of the ancient Israelites that, as they marched through the desert to the Chosen Land, they went family by family. This, of course, remains basically true for the new Israel, the Church, which marches through this earthly desert, family by family, toward the celestial kingdom. In the family and only there can the strength and roots of Christian life be fostered. This was true both of the old and the new covenant, as the nuptial blessing points out so well: "O God, who doth join man to woman, and give to that society, the first to be established, the blessing which alone was not taken away in punishment for original sin nor in the doom of the Flood; O God, who hast consecrated the union of marriage making it a sign so profound as to prefigure in the marriage covenant the mystery of Christ and the Church."[17]

We can safely say that the place of marriage as a means of sanctity in the lay apostolate will have to be emphasized even more in the future than in the past. We have already spoken of the sacred function of the parents in instructing their children in the rudiments of the faith. To this we must add that today, more than ever before, married couples are very anxious

---

[15] The Divine Milieu (New York, 1960), p. 33; also see the insights of W. Ong, Frontiers in American Catholicism (New York, 1960); in this regard laymen ought to make their own the prayer of the Third Sunday after Pentecost: "Sic transeamus per bona temporalia, ut non amittamus aeterna."

[16] There has been so much written in this regard that it is hard even to mention the best. See among the most recent J. Leclercq, Marriage: A Great Sacrament (New York, 1954); J. Guitton, Essay on Human Love (London, 1959); J. DeFabregues, Christian Marriage (New York, 1959); J. L. Thomas, The American Catholic Family (Westminster, Md., 1958); H. Caffarel, Love and Grace in Marriage (Notre Dame, Ind., 1960); L. Cervantes, And God Made Man and Woman (Chicago, 1959); etc.

[17] From the Collectio Rituum, p. 121.

to know how they can become saints in and through their marriage, not in spite of it. Theologians and spiritual writers have begun to answer this appeal by urging the establishment of the Christian Family Movement, Cana and Pre-Cana Conferences, special courses on the high school and college levels, family retreats, and special periodical literature dedicated to the family apostolate. The father, for instance, ought to watch with love over the well-being of his spouse and children and thus collaborate for the posterity of his country and his Church. These duties of parents have a sacred character. It is no easy task constantly to nourish love of the spouses for each other "as Christ loved the Church." It is possible only through a profound Christian understanding of the spiritual meaning of this great sacrament.

Some authors have sought to build this marital spirituality on the analogy of the three vows of obedience, poverty, and chastity. Others discourage this approach since the three vows were historically conceived in function of the religious life, which will always be their principal term of reference. As these authors point out, the religious life is the flowering and supreme fruit of marital love. It is a fact that the most vigorous religious vocations come from families where Christian and human love are abundant.[18] When Christian and human love does not flower in abundance, it is taxing belief that, in general, any divine vocation to the religious life will grow. Perhaps we should conclude this section with the wise observation of Canon Leclercq: fervent religious vocations come from deeply Christian families which nothing can supplant for this purpose, neither school nor Church. This fervent Christian family life, however, will be lived when the couples themselves realize the tremendous dignity and responsibility incumbent upon them in family life.

---

[18] See the sociological study of J. A. Fichter, *Religion as an Occupation* (Notre Dame, Ind., 1961), pp. 35–38; also see the interesting remarks of P. Carswell, *Offbeat Spirituality* (New York, 1961), pp. 49–65.

Various Concrete Developments

The lay apostolate has developed along many lines since its charter was granted. This many-sided evolution can be easily seen by glancing at the agenda for the two International Congresses for the lay apostolate held at Rome in 1951 and 1957.[19] In the following we wish to cover two of the more interesting areas which have meaning for laymen of our day. Every choice is a sacrifice, but since this chapter simply gives general orientations in the field of the lay apostolate, it seems justified to summarize two of its more interesting developments.

1. THEOLOGY OF WOMAN

The theology of woman has barely begun and yet is an area which has been given much thought by theologians.[20] The question is a rather new one but most important in view of the new status and responsibility that woman has attained in our day. Even the Popes have remarked on this subject, and an interesting collection of their works has been made by the monks of Solesmes.[21]

The question of woman's role was recently posed in a book by the French woman existentialist, Simone de Beauvoir.[22] After

---

[19] For the texts of the Congresses one should write to the Permanent Committee for International Congresses of the Lay Apostolate, Piazza S. Calisto 16, Rome, Italy. For a good résumé, see the chapter "The World of Today: The Responsibilities of the Laity," Laymen Face the World, II (Rome, 1958), pp. 255–278.

[20] F. A. Arnold, La Femme dans l'Eglise (Paris, 1955); H. Deutsch, The Psychology of Women (New York, 1958); D. Dohen, Women in Wonderland (New York, 1959); E. Firkel, Women in the Modern World (Chicago, 1956); J. Fitzsimons, Woman Today (New York, 1952); Writings of Edith Stein (Westminster, Md., 1956); The Vocation of the Single Woman, ed. A. M. Carre (New York, 1960); G. von le Fort, The Eternal Woman, rev. ed. (Milwaukee, 1962); B. Lavand, "Toward a Theology of Woman," The Thomist, 2 (1940), 460–474; H. Rondet, "Elements pour une théologie de la Femme," Rév. Nou. Théo., 79 (1957), 915–940; see also the very interesting chapter of J. Leclercq, "Woman in the Family and in Society," in his book Marriage and the Family (New York, 1949), pp. 291–349.

[21] The Woman in the Modern World, papal teaching (Boston, 1958).

[22] The Second Sex (New York, 1953). It is on the Index.

giving due credit to Christianity for all it has done for woman, she unleashes a veritable torrent against the "slaveries" into which men, and Christianity in particular, have relegated woman. Woman is passive, tied down both domestically and in her own body; she is encumbered in both her social and civil life. In reality, Madame de Beauvoir's is a vigorous protest against the very state of womanhood, the protest of a woman who, in reality, wants to be a man. But that is not to say that many of her criticisms are not to the point. Her invectives against the distorted conception of woman in some Christian circles, coming from a certain type of Augustinian tradition in matters of civil and economic inequality, are quite justified. But all this is beside the vital point: does woman as woman have a specific role to play in God's plan of redemption, and, if so, what are her possibilities within the confines of the proper spiritual, moral, psychological, and physiological structures which God has given her?

The history of woman in human institutions is too varied to be traced here, but one fact does emerge: woman has traditionally been treated as an inferior being to man. The great novelty of Christianity was to declare the absolute spiritual equality of man and woman before God.[23] This basic teaching results from a study of the texts of the Gospels and Epistles.[24] But the social repercussions of this aspect of Christian doctrine came about very slowly. This process of evolution is not strange to man, not even to Christian man. Such a progress of slow evolution is not an opportunistic adjustment to cultural change; it is a real growth in knowledge and understanding, aided by the Holy Spirit, of what has always been contained in revelation but hitherto imperfectly appreciated. These clearer insights frequently occur when historical changes reveal the cultural encrustations that have hidden an unrealized doctrinal truth. Neither this possibility nor the process of clarification should surpise, much less

---

[23] Cf. Gal 3:28: "In Christ Jesus there is no longer Jew and Greek, free man or slave, neither man nor woman." Cf. H. Rondet, art. cit., p. 916.

[24] Ibid., p. 926.

shock us: the founding Fathers for all their resounding belief
that "all men are created equal," decided in Section 2, article 1
of the Constitution that a Negro, still enslaved and disenfran-
chised, was to be counted as ⅗ of a person in assessing taxes
and apportioning seats in Congress. We now realize — and how
belatedly — that a Negro should have access to a state university,
even if it takes two Army divisions to do it. We could compare
the theology of woman in Christianity to this type of evolution.
It is unfortunate that it took so long, but let us not simply
lament history; let us examine its theological content.

The main role of women will always be motherhood, be it
spiritual or physical. Common sense dictates that without a
healthy family, great men are seldom born. To a very great degree, a man is what his mother has made him, and it is not
without some truth that "the hand that rocks the cradle rules
the world." In Christianity, however, this maternity is not restricted to the physical level. A Christian mother's role is
to form her children spiritually as well as physically, to lead
them to Christ. Moreover, there come to mind the thousands
of sacred virgins consecrated to the love of Christ without
whose service the Church of the modern world would indeed
be less rich: teachers and nurses, missionaries and social workers,
contemplatives and writers — all consecrated to the love of
Christ in and through their femininity.

But the social structures of society have changed. The dis-
course of Pius XII on October 21, 1945, is most significant.[25]
The Holy Father explains that while the main preoccupation
of women will always be the home, this is not for all women
and it must not remain their exclusive preoccupation. He wisely
points out that although woman is in no way inferior to man,[26]
she is complementary to him in her psychological, physiological,
and spiritual qualities, and this complementarity must be respected if she is to engage with profit in the new realm of action
open to her in the modern world. All efforts at a vulgar "equal-

---

[25] Text in *The Woman in the Modern World*, pp. 127–142.
[26] *Ibid.*, p. 134.

ity," or at reducing woman to performing the same tasks in the same way as men, must be avoided under pain of nullifying her apostolate.[27] The Holy Father goes even further: new social realization has awakened woman to the beneficial role she can play in the social and political field.[28] The Christian woman must engage in this role with resolution and with determination. Her beneficial mission has become, along with that of man, a necessary factor of civilization and progress.[29] But woman must bring this about in her own way, in conformity with the specific talents God has given her. Woman is essentially a mother and always will remain so. She must develop herself along the maternal lines of care for others, care for persons and not things, striving to bring about their happiness, becoming the cause of peace, seeking always the good of persons.[30] If she is physically weaker than man, she knows a strength which outdoes that of man at the bed of a sick person; her strength is different from his, and perhaps in the long run more useful. If she is generally incapable of complicated rationalization, she has a strong sense of the concrete good of individuals and persons rather than the power to conceive grandiose ideas and structures. Her qualities, therefore, are different from those of men and they must be respected if she is to contribute anything to the progress and history of mankind.

The tasks ready and open for her delicate qualities are really without number. The functions of teacher and nurse have always been a perfect choice for women because of their tender solicitude for children and the weak; women as psychologists are truly a remarkable group in almost instinctively and scientifically understanding the disturbances of children; as social workers they are without peers in the field of personal betterment of the groups with which they come in contact. The field of politics is certainly an open vocation where more women must participate. Women's sense of social justice, their personal responsibility, and their moral demands on society

[27] Ibid., p. 138.
[28] Ibid., p. 144.
[29] Ibid., p. 152.
[30] Ibid., p. 160.

are necessary factors which form a good counterbalance to the comparative coldness of "rational" men. Poetry, literature, and letters await the genius of women to bring out more beauty and order. All these functions, and this listing is by no means complete, are compatible with woman's essential maternal function. This is important to realize, for there are certain activities which are not compatible with her feminine nature. She is not naturally at home in a world of automation, and even the usual role of secretary involves her in solicitude for things rather than people. But these are practical problems which have to be worked out as time goes on. One thing, however, is certain: the role of today's Christian woman cannot be confined to the domestic scene; her limits are the ends of the earth, for she shares responsibility with man for the progress and good of humanity. But this progress will profit from woman's participation only if she recognizes what she is and what she has been given: since she is essentially a mother, she exists for the beneficial service of others. Her contribution, which is vital, must be along these lines under pain of her own self destruction.

2. FREE SPEECH IN THE CHURCH

The subject of free speech in the Church has been of great interest to theologians lately. A work by an Austrian theologian has recently opened up this field to the English-speaking public, a need which has long since been felt in American circles.[31] It is what Fr. Congar calls freedom "in the Church, but not with regard to the Church, that is to say, not with regard to the essential things of that institution which Jesus Christ founded for our salvation."[32] It represents a desire on the part of the faithful, at the suggestion of the Sovereign Pontiff himself, to

---

[31] K. Rahner, *Free Speech in the Church* (New York, 1959); Y. Congar, *Laity, Church and World* (Baltimore, 1960); I. Gorres, *Die Leibhaftige Kirche, Gesprach unter Laien* (Frankfurt, 1950); J. H. Newman, *On Consulting the Faithful in Matters of Doctrine* (New York, 1962); D. Zaehringer, "Besinnung und Ausschauung. Priester und Laien. Heilige Kirche," *Bened. Monatschrift*, 34 (1958), 58–64.

[32] Y. Congar, *op. cit.*, p. 42.

take an active interest in the affairs of the Church.[33] It is not a question of reinstituting the infamous "trusteeism" which darkened the pages of early American Church history;[34] nor does it represent a sort of vulgar democracy where all questions are settled by the fiat of the all-powerful majority. This desired interest on the part of the laity involves no contest with the authority of the hierarchy, neither with their teaching nor their sanctifying powers. It is simply a question of using the layman as a valuable channel of the Holy Spirit whom each of the faithful receives as a member of the Church. Priests and the hierarchy are not the only members of the Church who have received the Holy Spirit. All inspiration does not come from the priests and the hierarchy even though it is they who, in the final analysis, approve and give official sanction to this or that particular movement of the Spirit within the Church. There may be as much danger of neglecting or misunderstanding an authentic message sent by God through a layman as there is of receiving an imposter.

As far back as New Testament times we ascertain certain laymen charged with an evangelical message to be preached.[35] They were distinct from the hierarchy but not independent of it. For the New Testament, the charism of prophecy was not restricted to the hierarchy alone. We see this in St. Paul's First Epistle to the Corinthians (1 Cor 9:1). A prophet is simply one who speaks in the name of God. He who prophesizes addresses men in words of edification, exhortation, and consolation. Even women can be given this gift for the edification of the Church. The Didaché, one of the first documents of early Christianity, recognized that there can be official preachers of the world outside of the hierarchy. There is danger of imposters, but there is also the equal danger of rejecting a real charism. For this purpose, the Holy Spirit can raise up anyone in the Church

---

[33] Address of Pius XII to International Congress of the Press, AAS, 42 (1950), 256.

[34] See R. D. Cross, *The Emergence of Liberal Catholicism in America* (Cambridge, 1958), pp. 106–129.

[35] Lk 10:1–16; Mt 10:41.

as He has done time and again. All must be submitted to the official hierarchy for ultimate approval, but that does not mean that the Spirit cannot raise voices of protest, self-examination, etc., in the Church. The authority must listen and control; it has no right to disdain or set limits on what the Spirit can or cannot do.

In ancient times, this voice of the Spirit among the faithful was known as the *consensus fidelium* and is treated with respect by theologians in our own day.[36] In 1949, for example, Pope Pius XII sent to all the bishops of the Catholic Church a sort of questionnaire to inquire what they and their flocks thought of the dogma of the Assumption.

Our interest here, however, is not in matters of dogma but in a healthy spirit of self-criticism and evaluation of customs and institutions within the Church.[37] Criticism is not rebellious if it is done in a constructive and charitable spirit, but its existence is most necessary within the Church so that the authorities can come to recognize the authentic voice of the Spirit who can speak to them through the body of the faithful in general or by individuals in particular. Many times the proper authorities in the Church can only be enlightened in this way about the true nature of institutions and their usefulness or adaptability today.

Pius XII called this so necessary that "something would be lacking to her life were there no public opinion in it (the Church), a want for which the blame would rest on the pastors and the faithful."[38] And still stronger are the words of Cardinal Stritch: "Lay persons are not forbidden to protest against the shortcomings of members of the clergy, by a brotherly remonstrance and with a due sense of their own deficiencies."[39]

---

[36] J. H. Newman, *op. cit.*, pp. 53–71.

[37] See the interesting reactions in this regard to the book of Fr. Lombardi, *Il Concilio* (Rome, 1961), and the more balanced yet forceful work of H. Küng, *The Council, Reform, and Reunion* (New York, 1962).

[38] *AAS*, 42 (1950), 256.

[39] Address to the Catholic press in 1954 as quoted by R. C. Hartnett, "Public Opinion within the Church," *America*, 97 (1954), 315–317.

Yet a somewhat authoritarian clergy "often seem more ready to give orders than to educate, to insist than to uplift."[40] In the clergy's defense, however, we might add that many Catholics often try to shelter behind some authority, some law or decisions or extract from a papal document. Catholic laymen must first become "adults" with a right to independent opinions in their proper fields — art, culture, intellectual life, politics, music, professions, business world, etc., and articulate in matters of cultural and professional intelligence before they can presume to offer constructive criticism of the Church's problems.[41] But the layman has already progressed to a degree not suspected by some of the clergy, with the result that they treat the criticisms and observations of the educated laity as they would those of an adolescent.[42]

> Patience is necessary on both sides. The Church authorities must be patient, not regarding every frank expression of opinion or criticism as an attack upon themselves or on essential Church principles and institutions, or an attempt to outvote them and their decisions. Those under their authority must be patient, not giving the impression that they regard every admonition from above as an out-and-out attack upon free expression within the Church. . . .[43]

Many strides have been made. Fr. Lombardi has suggested a sort of council of educated laymen around each bishop to advise him on diverse matters affecting the Church.[44] Some American bishops have appointed permanent lay members to their liturgical commissions. Some dioceses have entrusted other labors in important areas to laymen, as in the case of the appointment of a layman as public-relations manager for the diocese. Who would know this field better than a layman? The writers of *Commonweal* have constituted their periodical as a forum for airing intelligent lay opinion in the Church of

---

[40] Y. Congar, *op. cit.*, p. 25; D. J. Thorman, "Laymen without Voices," *America*, 105 (1961), 252–254.

[41] K. Rahner, *op. cit.*, pp. 72, 74.

[42] *Ibid.*, p. 52.

[43] *Ibid.*, p. 39.

[44] *For a Better World* (Chicago, 1958), p. 176.

America.[45] In Canada, even many of the Catholic colleges and schools are placed in the hands of laymen. Perhaps this would leave religious more time to do what is essential to their religious vocations. One wonders why laymen cannot become principals of our Catholic parochial schools; laymen would be more acquainted with the specific home lives of children, secular activities into which children are to be integrated, besides giving fine example of married lay Christians as exemplary Catholics and educators. It is certainly a simple type of clericalism which would say that such posts "must" be given to priests or religious. These same observations could very easily be applied to other administrative positions as hospitals, Catholic charities, cemeteries, radio and television boards and, above all, the Catholic press. The time has come to give these thoughts serious consideration on the part of those concerned. Note, for instance, the words of Pope John XXIII to the 4000 Salesian lay "Cooperators," whom he "sincerely invited to take their place of responsibility as individuals and members of a community under the friendly guidance of the bishops and at the side of the priests in brotherly understanding" (Allocution of June 1, 1962).

Whatever organized structure may eventually be devised to channel lay opinion by the competent ecclesiastical authority, one thing is quite certain: the welfare of the whole Church is the responsibility of all, laymen and hierarchy alike, although this responsibility rests unequally on them. The old category of the morals books of the *peccatum tactiturnitatis* (failing to speak to enlighten a superior or when the common good is involved) must be revised and put into the layman's confessional guide.

Conclusion

The apostolate of the Church is one which continues un-

---

[45] In addition to *Commonweal, Cross Currents, Integrity, Catholic Worker, The Tablet* (English), *l'Esprit* (French) are important journals of opinion under the direction of laymen. *Integrity,* unfortunately, is now defunct, but its founder, the late Ed. Willock, did much to bring papal social teachings to the attention of all — lay and clergy.

changed through the centuries: to bring God's salvation to men and to their world. The application of this apostolate, however, becomes diverse because of the changing needs of the times. Our times are no exception and we can safely say that we are witnessing such revolutions in society as have not been surpassed in all the rest of history combined. To meet this new reality, the theology of the laity has been elaborated not as a temporary remedy but as a basic element of ecclesiology. The layman's position in the Church is to be the connecting link, the saving ferment in a world which does not know Christ. His spirituality, consequently, must be thought out in that perspective. The future only offers ever more and plentiful opportunities for the apostolic laymen in and of the Church.

Bibliographical Note

1. Anciaux, P. *Le Sacrément du Marriage.* Louvain: Ed. Nauwelaerts, 1961.

    Cited as one of the finest dogmatic, psychological, and spiritual syntheses of modern literature on the subject. His theme — and this work is cited only as exemplary — is that of sanctity in and through marriage as a vocation.

2. Arnold, F. X. *La Femme dans l'Eglise.* Paris: Ed. Ouvrieres, 1955.

    The theology of the place of woman in the Church and of her proper mission has received much attention from theologians of late. Here Arnold attempts to give such a synthesis in a way adapted to the changing role of woman in the Church, in the family, and in the world.

3. Barth, Karl. *Community, State and Church.* Garden City, N. Y.: Doubleday, 1960 (paperback).

    This is a Protestant work on the nature of Church-State relations. Cited here as exemplar along with the works of Congar, Murray, Rommen, etc. — on the great field open to laymen in these delicate matters.

4. Bordin, L. *La Participazione dei Fedeli al Sacrificio della Missa nella Teologia Contemporanea.* Rome, 1948.

    A rather broad summary of contemporary thought on the basis and structure of priesthood and the faithful in the sacrifice of the Mass. Somewhat outdated — but valuable bibliographical tool for earlier literature.

5. Botte, B., Charlier, A., Robeyns, A. *Le Sacerdoce des Fideles.* Louvain: 1934.

On the same lines as Bordin, but approaches the subject from a total view of the liturgy instead of just the Mass. Valuable insights for theology of participation of the faithful in the priesthood of Christ and His mission.

6. Caffarel, H. *Love and Grace in Marriage.* Notre Dame, Ind.: Fides, 1956.

Cited as exemplar of the modern effort to integrate the sacrament of marriage into the full life of the Church — its vocation and sublime dignity in the mystery of Christ's love.

7. Canals, S. *Secular Institutes and the State of Perfection: The Priesthood and the State of Perfection.* Chicago: Scepter Press, 1959.

One of the few books in English on the intrinsic meaning of the secular institutes in the religious life. It is more a legal thesis than anything else and can be profitable if used for this. The second part on the priesthood — especially with reference to the state of perfection — must be accepted with caution and reserve.

8. Cardijn, J. *Challenge to Action.* Chicago: Fides, 1955.

Essays and talks by the founder of the Young Christian Workers, on the nature of the lay apostolate — especially with reference to the meaning of labor and industry. Insights on an interpretation of the meaning of labor.

9. Carré, A. M., ed. *The Vocation of the Single Woman.* New York: P. J. Kenedy, 1960.

Various essays by outstanding laymen on the various Christian callings and works for the woman who wishes to consecrate herself to serving Christ in the world. Such themes as "at the disposal of our neighbor," "celibacy and professional life," "effects on society" will give reflection to the young girl who wishes to serve Christ outside of marriage and outside of the religious state.

10. Carswell, P. *Offbeat Spirituality.* New York: Sheed and Ward, 1961.

Interesting and humorous insights into the "spirituality" of the modern layman today — the "hows" and "whys" of his life and how to sanctify himself in and through them.

11. Casserlay, J. V. *The Bent World.* New York: Oxford University Press, 1955.

An interesting study by a Protestant theologian on the evils and pitfalls of Western civilization — its need for a revision and revival, concerning such fields as secularism in the West, divorce, economies, technology. It will prove refreshing for the layman.

12. A *Catholic Catechism*. New York: Herder & Herder, 1961.

This work, a sign of our times, integrates the whole course of Catholic catechetics in a more deeply steeped liturgical, biblical, and ecclesial foundation. Perfect preparation for all apostles — lay and religious. Cited as representing a general tendency today.

13. The Catholic Theological Society of America. *Proceedings of the 1959 Convention*, "The Theology of the Lay Apostolate," pp. 151–161.

About the most concise analysis in English of the lay apostolate — its objectives and theological foundations. Written from a dogmatic, theological point of view and with good bibliographical references.

14. Cerfaux, L. *The Church in the Theology of St. Paul*. New York: Herder & Herder, 1959.

To understand anything of the position of the layman in the Church, one must understand the very reality of what the Church is. Here Msgr. Cerfaux gives just such an analysis of St. Paul and his thought on the Church. Cited as exemplar along with the works on the Church by Congar, Mersch, De Lubac, De Montcheuil, etc.

15. Chenu, M. D. *Pour Une Théologie du Travail*. Paris: Ed. du Seuil, 1955.

Chenu has tried in this small book to give a theological interpretation to the notion of work taken in its broadest meaning — any creative activity of man as engagement of his personality, furthering creation, etc.

16. *Christian Asceticism and Modern Man*. London: Blackfriars Association, 1957.

The foundation governing Christian mortification remains the same for all Christians. But various conditions of man's life and activity condition its application. Here experts examine physiological, psychological, and anthropological factors of modern man and their application to the problem of Christian asceticism.

17. Coleburt, R. *The Search for Values*. New York: Sheed and Ward, 1960.

Essays on the function of Christian values as applied to various forms of man's activity — religious and secular. Coleburt gropes for the human and religious meaning of science and technology, intellectual pursuits, culture, and art.

18. Colomes, Luis. *The Church and Creation*. Paterson, N. J.: St. Anthony Guild Press, 1956.

Rather superficial interpretation and meaning of the created world in the Christian mystery. Its advantage is that it is one of the few sorely needed works in English on the subject.

19. Congar, Y. *Laity, Church and the World*. Baltimore: Helicon Press, 1960.

A series of three essays on the position of laymen with regard to their apostolate in the world. Notes on the history of the lay apostolate's freedom and his prophetical office make for good short readings.

20. Corte, N. *Pierre Teilhard de Chardin*. New York: Macmillan, 1960.

Cited only as one of the many works on this very important man today. Chardin's thought is probably one of the most penetrating on the discovery of meaning — the Christian meaning — of human progress as well as cosmic signification. Very important figure for laymen today. Here we have a short summary of his thought.

21. Dabin, P. *Le Sacerdoce Royal des Fideles dans la Tradition Ancienne et Moderne*. Bruxelles, 1950.

One of the most complete historical summaries of the question in print. Indispensable for any tradition analysis of the position of the layman in the Church in history. Modern trends and good bibliographies.

22. De Chardin, Pierre Teilhard. *The Phenomenon of Man*. New York: Harper, 1959.

23. ——— *The Divine Milieu*. New York: Harper, 1960.

Both works are indispensable reading for the education of the scholarly layman of today. These are but two of his works — other articles appear in periodical literature. De Chardin, along with Thils and Congar, endeavors to give a Christian interpretation of the full phenomenon of reality — visible reality — the cosmos and its center, man. His works are *sub judicio* — but no one can question his importance today in the world of progress, science, and technology.

24. De Montcheuil, Y. *Aspects of the Church*. Chicago: Fides, 1955.

Comprehensive work on the diverse manifestations of the Church with regard to its internal and external life — in the Church and in the world. The temporal order, Church-State problems, missions, and the Mystical Body are all discussed clearly and, in some chapters, with original insight.

25. ——— *For Men of Action*. Chicago: Fides, 1956.

Excellent short treatise on the specific functions of laymen and of Catholic action in general in the Church. De Montcheuil gets down to particulars, and this makes his work all the more valuable.

26. ———— *Guide for Social Action*. Chicago: Fides, 1954.

Much food for laymen engaged in the active field of Catholic lay apostolate in politics, business, intellectual pursuits, etc. Valuable insights into a Christian interpretation.

27. Dohen, D. *The Layman's Spirituality*. New York: Sheed and Ward. 1954.

One of the first books on this subject in English, written in a pleasant style. Its basic theme is that the layman's spirituality cannot be that of a "watered-down" religious endeavor similar to priests and nuns. The Christian laws of perfection apply to all indiscriminately, but they must be applied differently to the layman of our times.

28. Dondeyne, A. *Contemporary European Thought and Christian Faith*. Pittsburgh: Duquesne University Press, 1958.

Thoughts for confrontation of modern existential currents — both pagan and Christian — and Christian faith. Extremely important for understanding many currents of modern thought — essential for the layman in the Church and in the world he must penetrate.

29. Dooley, T. A. *The Night They Burned the Mountain*. New York: Farrar, Straus & Cudahy, 1960.

30. ———— *Deliver us from Evil*. New York: Farrar, Straus & Cudahy, 1959.

31. ———— *The Edge of Tomorrow*. New York: Farrar, Straus & Cudahy, 1959.

The story of one courageous layman — in this case a doctor — and his struggles against human misery, disease, and death in a country where there is only one doctor for 150,000 people. A great source of encouragement for our dedicated laymen who are doing God's work in the world.

32. Eliade, M. *The Sacred and the Profane*. New York: Harcourt, Brace and Co., 1959.

A general work on the interdependency or rather distinction and interaction of the religious-worldly realities and their effects on each other. Philosophical in tone, the work is useful, even excellent, in grasping the question of the distinction and dependency of the two fundamental realities of Christianity.

33. Ellis, J. T. *American Catholics and the Intellectual Life*. Chicago: Heritage Foundation, 1956.

The "bomb" which has set off Catholic controversy since its publication. Ellis claims that Catholics have not by far contributed their share to the intellectual life in any field in the United States.

His accusation of anti-intellectualism of American Catholicism was particularly felt in Catholic circles.

34. Folliet, J. *World Catholicism Today*. Westminster, Md.: Newman, 1961.

Interesting essays on the problems of Catholicism in the modern age. Problems such as modern technology, lay spirituality, social movement today are discussed very appropriately and convincingly. Intended for the layman and the confrontation of his problem.

35. Fournier, R. *La Théologie de l'Action Catholique*. Montreal: Major Seminary, 1940.

Rather old and outdated today — but valuable from a bibliographical point of view, especially with regard to pontifical documents and their context.

36. Gardiner, H. D. *Norms for the Novel*. Garden City, N. Y.: Hanover House, 1960.

Discusses delicate matters of censorship, obscenity, and moral and artistic evaluation of creative literature. Valuable for the lay writer and reader and concerns one of those fields — censorship — open to public discussion today. See also Fr. Gardiner's *Catholic Viewpoint on Censorship* (Hanover House, 1959) — an excellent contribution.

37. Geaney, D. J. *Christians in a Changing World*. Chicago: Fides, 1959.

As with other writers on the same subject cited above, Geaney tries to give a Christian orientation to the various and new situation of Catholic laymen in the United States. Valuable insights into "lay spirituality."

37a. Gerken, John, S.J., *Toward a Theology of the Layman*. New York: Herder & Herder, 1963.

A brilliant and controversial presentation of Fr. Rahner's position. Part I, on the state of the layman, argues that the lay state is not less perfect than the religious; Part II presents an existential ethics for the laity.

38. Glazer, N., and McEntire, D., eds. *Studies in Housing and Minority Groups*. Santa Barbara, Calif.: University of California Press, 1960.

One of the three definitive studies issued by the Commission on Race and Housing, this volume contains seven studies on the housing of Negroes, Mexican-Americans, Puerto Ricans, Japanese-Americans, and smaller minority groups which define the range and complexity of a major problem confronting our Catholic laymen as citizens and as Christians.

39. Gleason, R. W. *Christ and the Christian.* New York: Sheed and Ward, 1959.

A sort of general spirituality — or rather basic spirituality based on the essentials of Christianity — whether he be religious or lay. Humility, suffering, fear, hope, and love are treated with a scriptural, psychological, and traditional insight uncommon in most modern writers.

40. Guardini, R. *The Faith and Modern Man.* London: Burns, Oates, 1953.

The difficulties experienced by modern man are not only different but even more dangerous than those of ages past. Intellectually, it is more diifficult today to give assent to faith than in past times. The difficulties of modern man are here faced and answered.

41. Guerry, Bishop. *l'Eglise et la Communanté des Peuples.* Paris: Ed. Bonne Press, 1958.

A fine synthesis on the moral obligation for Catholics to take a formal share in international community — mostly from the teachings of the Popes — particularly Pope Pius XII.

42. ———— *The Social Doctrine of the Church.* New York: Alba House, 1962.

This is but one work of many in the field of social justice. It pinpoints a great field of endeavor for consecrated laymen — even laymen and their families (cf. AID which takes whole families which live together for two to five years). Follows the theme of Pius XI — you must humanize before you Christianize. This social consciousness is here emphasized with clear exposition and vigor.

43. Haley, J. F., ed. *Apostolic Sanctity in the World.* Notre Dame, Ind.: University of Notre Dame Press, 1956.

Mostly a series of essays on the nature and meaning for the Christian community of secular institutes. The difficulties proper to such institutes are openly discussed along with their unlimited opportunities for good.

44. Häring, B. *The Law of Christ,* Vol. I. Westminster, Md.: Newman, 1961, Vol. II, 1963.

Häring examines new tendencies in moral theology in its approach to a more positive living of the Christian reality. This excellent book stems from a desire to give and form all relations to God and men in the unique light of the love of Christ. Along with G. Gilleman's *The Primacy of Charity in Moral Theology* (Newman, 1960), this represents an excellent trend away from the somewhat negative moral teachings for laymen of the past.

45. Hesburgh, T. M. *The Relation of the Sacramental Characters of*

Baptism and Confirmation to the Lay Apostolate. Washington, D. C.: Catholic University of America Press, 1946.

An interesting analysis of the history and theology of the sacraments of baptism and confirmation and their implications in the life of all the baptized. Aged, but good bibliography.

46. Humman, A. *La Rédemption et l'Ordre Social Chrétienne.* Paris: Plon, 1949.

Excellent essays on the meaning and implication of the total Christian redemption and its effects and repercussions on the whole of the social Christian order — work, employment, progress, etc.

47. Kavang, W. A. *Lay Participation in Christ's Priesthood.* Washington, D. C.: Catholic University of America Press, 1935.

One of the first English treatises on the subject, it is mainly of historical interest now.

48. Lawler, J. G. *The Catholic Dimension in Higher Education.* Westminster, Md.: Newman, 1959.

Excellent essay in criticism and on the task and vocation of the Catholic intellectual. Interesting chapter on the layman's role in regard to the conquest of truth and his own proper vocation. Stresses scholarship as a Christian vocation in and for itself.

49. *The Lay Apostolate.* Papal teaching. Boston: St. Paul Editions, 1960.

Excellent résumé in English of all the teaching of the Popes from Leo XIII to Pius XII on the lay apostolate. Its index makes the work all the more valuable, since the documents can be traced chronologically, systematically, or alphabetically.

50. *Laymen in the Church.* Texts from the Second World Council for the Lay Apostolate. Rome: Ed. by the Permanent Committee for the Lay Apostolate, 1958. 3 vols.

51. Leclercq, Jacques. *Faith and Intelligence.* London: Burns, Oates, 1954.

Small but excellent résumé of the principal difficulties faced by modern man in his proper station. Valuable for understanding modern man's proper difficulties and for offering a partial Christian solution.

52. ———— *Christians in the World.* New York: Sheed and Ward, 1961.

Excellent, but somewhat biting, treatise on the history, meaning, and spirituality of the lay apostolate. Ideally written for the layman with no pretense to high scholarship.

53. *Leisure Living.* A series of lectures. Pittsburgh: Duquesne University, 1959.

One of the few works in English on a crying need of the American scene. These lectures offer historical background as well as some valuable insights on the new and creative use of more and more free time by workers in all areas.

54. Lippmann, W. *The Public Philosophy.* New York: The New American Library, 1959.

An interesting essay on political philosophy of democratic government and procedures, its basic foundation and structure. This represents one of the finest and clearest analyses of the need for fundamental principles if we are to survive as a democracy. Most interesting for the Catholic layman in the political field. See also Lippmann's brilliant *Public Opinion* (New York: Macmillan paperback, 1960), on force, power, news, censorship, economics, etc., in a free society.

55. Lombardi, R. *For a Better World.* Chicago: Fides, 1958.

Basic and very practical suggestions for work for the layman in the world. The work has been translated into ten languages and makes excellent food for thought for priests who want to see the "practical" application and value of the lay apostolate to the world.

56. MacDonald, D. *Catholics in Conversation.* Philadelphia: J. B. Lippincott, 1960.

A group of outstanding American Catholics in various fields are interviewed and questioned on the meaning and direction of their particular fields. Engaging conversations on such subjects as politics, liturgy, Church-State relationships, foreign aid, race relations, intellectual apostolate will render vital and real the vocation of laymen in these fields.

57. McAvoy, T. T., ed. *Roman Catholicism and the American Way of Life.* Notre Dame, Ind.: University of Notre Dame, 1960.

A self-critical examination by Catholic spokesmen analyzes the historical, political, and social position of Catholics in the United States, stressing the present religious situation and the changes which have taken place in Catholic American national groups.

58. McCarthy, E. J. *Frontiers in American Democracy.* Cleveland: The World Publishing Co., 1960.

A Catholic political figure gives his views on the political situation in the United States. His views, which cover such subjects as morality in politics, the meaning of the body politic, and civil liberties are strikingly Christian and Catholic.

59. March, Sabater. *Teologia del Apostolato de los Seglares Y Religiosos Laicos: Gracie Y Carisonas en la Accion Catolica.* Barcelona, Herder, 1958.

Spanish essays on the nature of both lay and religious apostolates in the world of today. March's comparison of the two states, and their limitations and advantages for Catholic action is valuable. Especially instructive for those who think that laymen are mere supplements to priests and nuns.

60. Maritain, J. *Man and the State.* Chicago: University of Chicago Press, 1951.

Interesting essays by one of the foremost lay Catholic thinkers today on the problems of the relationship between man and the State, with attention focused on his rights and obligations. Maritain applies the principles of natural law to political thinking in an original and creative way. More work along these lines is needed in a society dominated more and more by secularistic thought. The field is wide open for spirited laymen.

61. Masure, E. *The Sacrifice of the Mystical Body.* London: Burns, Oates, 1954.

A theological treatise on the part of the Mystical Body — the whole Church of the baptized — in the one unique sacrifice. Masure explains well the part, the position and dignity, of each member of the Church in offering as a single body the sacrifice of Christ.

62. Michlem, P. A. *The Secular and the Sacred.* London: Hodder and Stoughton, 1948.

In much the same way as Eliade, Michlem tries to establish the distinction and interdependency of these two realities in the Christian order. Interesting from the point of view of his explanation of the temporal order.

63. Michonneau, G., and Meurice, R. *Catholic Action and the Parish.* Westminster, Md.: Newman, 1955.

Various essays on the diverse functions of Catholic groups within the parish by two outstanding French pastors of the famous community of St. Severin. Interesting insights for parish priests.

64. Moehler, C. *Humanisme et Sainteté.* Paris, 1954.

One of the finest treatises on the fullness of the arts, culture, etc., as a part of the divine vocation of redemption. Most helpful for the layman who wishes to see some Christian meaning in his "profane" activities.

65. Mouroux, J. *I Believe.* New York: Sheed and Ward, 1959.

A very concise but valuable volume on the notion of faith in its spiritual as well as psychological aspects. Very helpful for the educated layman in seeing the meaning and connotation of faith in his life.

66. Murphy, J. F. *The Moral Obligation of the Individual to Partici-*

pate in *Catholic Action*. Washington, D. C.: Catholic University
of America Press, 1958.

An interesting treatise taken mostly from papal documents. The
author puts, perhaps, too much emphasis on the "moral" obligation
involved. Were the nature of this obligation as a necessary effect
of baptism and confirmation stressed instead, the work would be
improved.

67. Murray, T. E. *Nuclear Policy for War and Peace*. Cleveland: The
World Publishing Co., 1960.

Cited here both as an exemplar of what an educated Catholic
layman can do and as a positive contribution to the vexing and
disturbing problem of atomic energy. Formerly Commissioner of
the AEC, Murray treats in a profoundly Christian way the question
of disarmament, testing, and the moral use of this terrible force.
A great Christian contribution to the public forum.

68. Nagle, W. J., ed. *Morality and Modern Warfare*. Baltimore:
Helicon Press, 1960.

Interesting essays on the morality of modern atomic war and
its relation to the natural law. Will serve as a valuable contribution
to a problem which occupies the public (and Catholic) conscience
more than ever. Included is a valuable and complete bibliography.

69. Newman, J. *What is Catholic Action?* Westminster, Md.: Newman, 1958.

A well-rounded series of essays on the nature of the lay apostolate,
its aims, and the diverse forms which it takes in actual practice.
It can serve as a valuable introduction to the basic notions — fully
documented with papal texts.

70. O'Dea, T. F. *American Catholic Dilemma*. New York: Sheed and
Ward, 1958. Mentor Omega paperback, 1962.

A provocative essay, following and to a degree continuing the
essay by Msgr. Ellis. O'Dea shows why the intellectual movement
has not produced good results among American Catholics, discusses
the relation between faith and reason, and stresses the apostolate
involved in the attaining of truth.

71. Odegard, P. H. *Religion and Politics*. New York: Oceana Publications, 1960.

A unique reference work of selected statements on the relation
of religion to American politics, drawing upon various documents
from colonial times to the present. The editor, chairman of the
Department of Political Science at the University of California,
presents two chapters of very critical analysis on Catholicism as an
issue in politics.

72. *The Official Handbook of the Legion of Mary*, ed. by the Concilium Legionis Mariae. Louisville, Ky.: Publishers Printing Co., 1957.

　　Contains many valuable documents by various outstanding members of the Legion as well as pontifical texts on the nature and reason of the lay apostolate in general and the Legion in particular.

73. Orlandis, J. *The Christian in the World*. Chicago: Scepter Press, 1960.

　　Short and very popular work on the meaning of the world and its problems for the layman of today. Very elementary in scope, it can serve as a general introduction to further, more detailed reading.

74. Ortega y Gasset, J. *The Revolt of the Masses*. New York: W. W. Norton Co., 1957.

　　Best seller for over a year, Ortega's work gives a fine analysis of the change from Old-World thought patterns to contemporary views, and the tremendous repercussion of the latter on the modern mind and its direction. He attacks depersonalization and dehumanization in the technological age and gives some concrete approaches to the problem. Very important for understanding the modern mind.

75. Otto, R. *The Idea of the Holy*. New York: Oxford University Press, 1958.

　　Very ingenious insights into the nature of the sacred and divine in human realities — religion as well as art, sin, emotions, etc. Cited as a valuable contribution in the study of relationship between the temporal and the sacred.

76. Perrin, A. M. *Christian Perfection and Married Life*. Westminster, Md.: Newman, 1958.

　　One of the finer analyses of the possibility and the appropriateness of perfection in and through married life, embraced as a holy state in the Christian reality. Valuable, practical insights as to how this can be done concretely.

77. ——— *Forward the Layman*. Westminster, Md.: Newman, 1956.

　　General work on the nature, purpose, and foundation of the lay apostolate. Especially valuable is the concrete plan of action relative to the economic, missionary, and daily realities of the layman's life and work.

78. ——— *Secular Institutes*. New York: P. J. Kenedy, 1961.

　　Explains the need, foundation, and specific apostolate of such institutes. Perrin explains well the added difficulty or danger of being rejected both by the layman and the religious. Pontifical documents included.

79. Philips, G. *The Role of the Laity in the Church*. Cork: The Mercier Press, 1956.

Valuable and comprehensive study of the laity. With the work of Fr. Congar, this is "must" reading for anyone interested in the question. Covers everything from lay spirituality to the diverse forms of apostolic action.

80. Pika, E., ed. *Who is My Neighbor?* Greenwich, Conn.: Seabury Press, 1960.

"My neighbor" is the ex-convict, the derelict, the alcoholic, the individual who cannot afford medical or legal care, the old person, the refugee, and the physically and socially handicapped. The problems of these and other underprivileged minorities are discussed by fifteen humanitarians who have devoted their lives to the alleviation of human suffering. Great source of edification for Catholic laymen.

81. Rahner, K. *Free Speech in the Church*. New York: Herder & Herder, 1960.

Excellent treatise on the function and nature of criticism in the Church — especially by the layman. Obsequious silence can be just as bad as open rebellion. Includes practical plan of suggestions.

82. Rea, J. *The Common Priesthood of the Members of the Mystical Body*. Westminster, Md.: Newman, 1947.

Rather dated now, but still somewhat valuable for the understanding of the Thomistic principles of the notion of priesthood and its application to all the members of the Church.

83. Regamey, P. *Non Violence et Conscience Chrétienne*. Paris: Ed. du Cerf, 1958.

One of the foremost Catholic theologians on the contemporary scene speaks here on the thorny problem of war and peace. Responsibility, power, etc., also have their place — and both sides of the problem are given a sympathetic understanding. The case for Catholic pacificism.

84. ———— *The Cross and the Christian*. St. Louis: B. Herder Book Co., 1954.

To understand the work of redeeming the world and the participation in this work by the layman, the role of redemptive suffering, a necessary concomittant to every Christian reality, must be known. Regamey is especially good in showing the connection between suffering and redemption.

85. Reinhold, H. A. *Bringing the Mass to the People*. New York: Macmillan, 1960.

86. ———— *The Dynamics of the Liturgy*. New York: Macmillan, 1961.

Both of these works were written by a great apostle of the liturgy in America. His efforts here — and elsewhere — have been to make the average Catholic layman realize the great value and importance of the liturgy in his life by bringing home to him the meaning of the liturgy in his daily life.

87. Rideau, E. *Paganisme ou Christianisme*. Tournai: Casterman, 1954.

Modern analysis of the meaning of modern thought (particularly existentialism) for Christianity. Analyzes over twenty-five modern thinkers giving their basic thought and an interpretation. Discusses figures from both the Christian and non-Christian camp. While pointing to the need of understanding contemporary developments, Rideau points out that only Christianity can give a final answer.

88. Rondet, H. *Introduction à l'Etude de la Théologie du Marriage*. Paris: P. Lethielleux, 1959.

Excellent little volume tracing in broad outlines the history of the sacrament (canonical aspects as well) and the meaning of (Christian) marriage. Its bibliographical information and references make the work indispensable for anyone wishing to do work along these lines.

89. *Secular Institutes*. A Symposium on the Modern Lay Community. London: Blackfriars, 1952.

Various essays on the nature, responsibilities, and meaning of the new entity called the secular institute. Of special importance are two or three essays which show the acute difficulties which the movement is going through today.

90. Scheeben, M. J. *The Mysteries of Christianity*. St. Louis: B. Herder Book Co., 1938.

Cited for its emphasis on the Christological character of the sacraments and for the author's vital notions on the Church as the Mystical Body of Christ. Scheeben was among the first to emphasize new trends in ecclesiology.

91. Schwarz, B. V., ed. *The Human Person and the World of Values*. New York: Fordham University Press, 1960.

Various essays on diverse human goods in relation to their ultimate destinies — love — philosophy — time — truth, etc.

92. Shuster, G. N., ed. *Catholicism in America*. New York: Harcourt, Brace and Co., 1954.

Originally a series of important articles chosen from the Catholic lay magazine, *Commonweal*. Essential for determining the future march of Catholic laymen in the United States. Such subjects as social reform, education, politics, isolationalism, Jews, art, writing, science — subjects of vital concern to the lay apostolate — are covered.

93. Speaiglit, R. *Christian Theatre*. New York: Hawthorn Books, 1960.
A small popular work on the history, meaning, and development of the Christian art of the theatre.

94. Suenens, L. J. *Love and Control*. Westminster, Md.: Newman, 1961.
A very important work on the various difficulties and problems which face Catholic families today: divorce, birth control, free love, problems of self-mastery and love. The essential thesis is that love and sacrifice are both deep lessons of marriage, and that without them marriage problems even among Catholics will become even worse.

95. ——— *The Gospel to Every Creature*. Westminster, Md.: Newman, 1957.
Excellent little work on the need for direct training and preparation of lay apostles in their proper fields. The problems of the temporal vs. the eternal are very well treated in the chapter "To Humanize or to Evangelize?"

96. ——— *Theology of the Apostolate of the Legion of Mary*. Westminster, Md.: Newman, 1953.
A small treatise by an expert in the field on the important specialization of the lay apostolate, the Legion of Mary. With the Legion becoming more and more popular in our parishes, every parish priest would profit from Suenens' remarks.

97. Supreel, E. *Deux Essais sur le Progres*. Bruxelles: M. LeMertin, 1928.
Rather dated now, but still one of the first and better Christian interpretations of progress and technology. Supreel traces the thought in Scripture, tradition, and theology. His work remains a good reference for reading on the subject.

98. Tavard, G. *The Church, the Layman and the Modern World*. New York: Macmillan, 1959.
Excellent essays on the temporal role of the layman in the world as his proper vocation in the Church. Tavard touches not only the Catholic community in its relation to the state, but also technology, politics, and the mission of the Catholic to the non-Catholic world.

99. Thils, G. *Christian Attitudes*. Chicago: Scepter, 1959.
A very interesting essay on the two diverse Christian attitudes to the world and its proper reality: one, incarnationalism, uses earthly goods and gives them a Christian meaning and value; the other, eschatologicalism, uses the world but does not give it any meaning other than its proper finality.

100. ——— *Christian Holiness*. Tielt (Belgium): Ed. Lamoo, 1961.

Excellent treatise on ascetical and mystical theology of the total Christian reality. Laymen especially will profit from the chapters on the call to sanctity for all, the universalism of sanctity, and its specific manifestations in life.

101. Tillmann, F. *The Master Calls.* A handbook of morals for the layman. Baltimore: Helicon, 1960.

A very excellent treatise on the approach to moral theology from the positive point of view — as the very following of Christ based on Scripture. Divided into sections according to proper relationships — it is similar, although shorter, to Häring.

102. Tromp, S. *De Laicorum Apostolatus Fundamento, Indole, Formis.* (Pro Manuscr.) Roma: 1956.

Mimeographed notes on the foundation, justification, and objective of the lay apostolate today. Valuable as a source of a wealth of bibliographical materials.

103. Unger, D. J. *The Mystery of Love for the Single.* Chicago: Franciscan Herald Press, 1958.

In a series of well-chosen articles, Unger gives the necessity and the dignity of such a vocation in the world. Underlines dangers in this regard and gives some practical suggestions as to how to overcome them (chastity and modesty). It is more of a personal justification of the vocation itself rather than a deep analysis of the vocation with reference to the temporal world.

104. Van Kersbergen, L. *The Normal School of Sanctity for the Laity.* Grailville, Ohio: 1950.

A short, rather superficial, brochure on the engagement in the world and its tasks by the layman. The work was written mostly for Grail, the now famous lay missionary society. Interesting from the point of view of its missionary endeavor.

105. Vialatoux, J. *Morale et Politique.* Paris: Desclée de Brouwer, 1951.

Analyzes the Christian and moral aspects of political life, with a good deal of history. Valuable for the outlook of the lay Catholic as he enters the political field.

106. ———— *Signification Humaine du Travail.* Paris: Les Editions Ouvrieres, 1953.

Analyzes various theories of the meaning and signification of work and the sociological factors which influence it. A final analysis is given of the necessity, duty, right, and finality of work within the context of the Christian reality. A "must" for laymen in labor fields.

107. Von Balthasar, H. U. *Science, Religion and Christianity.* Westminster, Md.: Newman, 1958.

An excellent approach to a theological interpretation of matter, the cosmos, and terrestrial realities. The chapter, "The Sacrament of the Brother," where the need for fraternal charity is brought out in its full Christian contours, is especially interesting.

108. Von Le Fort, G. *The Eternal Woman*, rev. ed. Milwaukee: Bruce, 1962; *The Woman in the Modern World*. Papal teaching. Boston: St. Paul Editions, 1959; Evdokimov, P. *La Femme et le Salut du Monde*. Tournai-Paris: Desclée, 1958.

Three works of outstanding value which go to make up the beginning of a theology of the changed position of the woman not only in secular life but religious and ecclesial life as well. Her potentials are to be realized today more than ever before, given her advanced political, social and economic status. Never in the history of man has woman come to her own; never before, too, can she be an instrument for so much good or evil. Theologians today are trying to give a fuller mission to her role in Christianity. See also the excellent article by H. Rondet in *Nouvelle Révue Théologique*: "Elements pour une Théologie de la Femme," LXXIX (1957), 915–940, for rather complete bibliography. Also see *Lumière et Vie*, XLIII (1959): "Conception Chrétienne de la Femme."

109. Ward, Leo. *Catholic Life, U.S.A.; Contemporary Lay Movement*. St. Louis: Herder, 1959.

Fr. Ward offers an intimate view of the varied activities of Catholic lay organizations and indicates the impact they have on cultural and religious life of the country.

110. *Work: A Symposium*. London: Darton, Longman and Todd, 1960.

Diverse views on the meaning, direction, and humanization of human labor.

111. *World Crisis and the Catholic*. Published on the occasion of the Second World Congress for the Lay Apostolate. New York: Sheed and Ward, 1958.

A series of very interesting articles by Catholic laymen on science and technology, art, international community, and the responsibilities of the Catholic in each of these groups. Very informative as to the temporal realm of the layman.

112. Wyszynski, H. E. Cardinal. *Work*. London: Scepter Press, 1955.

A series of minor essays on the dignity and vocation of labor in the Christian context of creation and redemption.

SPECIAL STUDIES AND REPORTS

L'Apostolado dei Laici. Bibliographia Sistematica. Milano: Vita e Pensiero, 1957.

A valuable bibliography of some 2229 titles on the lay apostolate.
D'Arcy, M. C. *The Meaning and the Matter of History*. New York:
Farrar, Straus and Cudahy, 1959.

Cited as one of the finest efforts by a Christian to face problems
of today. It confronts dialectic materialism, communism, evolution,
etc. The Christian has a global view of history and its interpretation. Philosophically and theologically much still needs to be done
here.

Faith, Reason and Modern Psychiatry. New York: P. J. Kenedy,
1955; VanderVeldt, J. H., and Odenwald, R. P. *Psychiatry and
Catholicism*. New York: McGraw-Hill, 1957; Gleason, R. W., and
Hagmaier, G. *Counselling the Catholic*. New York: Sheed and
Ward, 1959.

These volumes highlight the work open to the Catholic medical
student and counselor. Many books have been written on these
subjects, but much more needs to be done — and Catholics have
not given their share in the field. These books will help to view
this great and open field as a vocation for many of our young
Catholic educated laymen.

Kraemer, H. *A Theology of the Laity*. Hulsean Lectures. London,
1958.

Interesting in that it was written by a Protestant for Protestants.
Note that we share many problems with our "Separated Brethren."

Leclercq, Jacques. *Back to Jesus*. New York: P. J. Kenedy, 1959.

A very interesting group of essays on the essence of Christian
perfection — not for any one particular group — but for the common calling of all. See especially the chapter on the Christian view
of the world and man.

Lumière et Vie. See some of the numbers of this journal totally
consecrated to various themes pertaining to the lay apostolate and
its mission. Among these are: *Reflections sur le Travail*, XX (1955);
Suicide et Euthanasie, XXXII (1957); *La Guerre*, XXXVIII
(1958); *L'Argent*, XXXIX, XLII (1958–59); *Vivre dans le Monde*,
L (1960).

Rommen, H. A. *The Natural Law*. St. Louis: B. Herder Book Co.,
1957.

Nothing is so troubling today between the Catholic and non-
Catholic camps as the notion of the natural law. Here Rommen
attempts to state the Catholic position in clear terms, tracing first
its history and then giving the elements of the philosophy and
content of the natural law.

PART III

THE CATHOLIC AND RELIGIOUS FREEDOM

INTRODUCTION

Of all the orientations of modern Catholic thought, none has more interest among both Catholics and non-Catholics than that of tolerance and religious freedom. A whole theological literature has been born in the past 25 years on this subject alone.[1] Nor is this discussion on tolerance and religious liberty restricted to Europe; in America as well, where Catholics are emerging to power in the economic and political fields, this is the subject of intense interest, reaching an almost hysterical tone among certain non-Catholic groups. During the 1960 presidential election the question of tolerance even appeared, at times, to take precedence over political issues.[2] At least it seemed to be so to the average Catholic in America. Many Catholics in the United States are becoming impatient with the line of argumentation which identifies the Church with totalitarian regimes of intolerance. American Catholics are tired of constant suspicions raised about their adherence to the Constitution and the American civil tradition. They are weary of the insinuation that Catholics hypocritically accept the First Amendment until they achieve such overwhelming political power that they can "establish" the Church, of the periodical warnings of Baptist conventions against "Roman" tendencies in American political spheres.[3]

Because of these and many other factors, the notion of tolerance in Catholic tradition has become a grave source of

[1] Cf. R. Aubert, *La Théologie Catholique au milieu du XXᵉ Siècle* (Tournai, 1954).

[2] Cf. titles dealing with this problem in the Bibliographical Note for this section, pp. 189–192.

[3] *Church-State Relations*, G. Weigel (Baltimore, 1960).

concern for theologians on both sides of the Atlantic. While American theologians have preferred to attack the problem from a civic and legal point of view, European theologians have considered it in a fully theological context and argumentation. For the first group, it is sufficient to safeguard the rights of conscience by civil and canon laws; for the second group, religious freedom is rooted in the notion of the sacredness of the human person and is disclosed by a strict analysis of the concept of faith as a response to God.

Yet why should there be any difficulty in the notion of religious freedom? There seems to be two difficulties which flow one from the other: one doctrinal, the other practical. It is well known that the Roman Catholic Church makes the exclusive claim that she and she alone has the total and essential deposit of religious truth which was given her by her divine Founder. In other words, she makes claim to be the true Church and representative of God on earth to the exclusion of all others. She is the community of salvation on earth, and outside of her unique fold there can be no salvation, no grace. She has been entrusted with all of the truths of faith by her divine Founder, and all other religions, Christian or pagan, are simply in error to the degree in which they differ from her on doctrinal matters.

Since this is so, certain Catholic theologians have argued that the Catholic Church alone has a strict right to exist. For, they claim, "error has no rights." Although Church and State are distinct societies by reason of their proper ends, these theologians hold that the duty of a "Catholic" state is to further the ends of the ecclesiastical society since the inferior society must aid the superior by virtue of the dignity of objectives.[4] The argument runs something like this: the State is a society which is both necessary and juridically perfect in the natural order. Since it is a perfect society (i.e., a society which fulfills man's needs in a certain order) it cannot be directly subordi-

---

[4] For argumentation in this respect, see F. G. Martinez, *Naturaleza jurídica y derechos de la Iglesia* (Pamplona, 1954), pp. 20–36; also note the speech of Cardinal Ottaviani in *l'Osservatore Romano* for March 4, 1953.

nated to any other society. This same notion of "perfect society" is consequently applied to the Church, and the result is that each power is supreme in its own order. Yet the Church does have a triple superiority to the State in that she is superior in dignity, magisterium, and jurisdiction. Because of this, the State must be at least indirectly subordinate to the Church, since the Church alone has the infallible magisterium to judge moral elements in society which indirectly affect the body temporal. There are two major theories regarding the subordination of the State to the Church. The one, upheld by Suarez and St. Robert Bellarmine, is known as the theory of indirect subordination;[5] the other is known as the moral theory or as the "thesis-hypothesis" theory. The theory of indirect subordination claims that in particular circumstances, when the realization of the Church's supernatural end demands, the Church can impose orders on the State with a true power of jurisdiction. If the State refuses to obey the Church in such circumstances, a real injustice is committed. In the moral theory, the power of the magisterium is exercised over all men since the Church is empowered by God to judge the morality of all human acts within the natural law. This power over nonreligious matters is a true power, but a moral one. According to this view, the Church does not impose any new precepts, but simply declares what is imposed by the moral and natural law in certain circumstances.

Since the end of the Church (salvation) is the supreme end of all men and institutions (so the moral argument goes), the State has a moral obligation to help the Church attain its end. Indirectly, it must repress heresies since these spiritual errors are very detrimental to the one, true faith. This system of concord or union, as it is commonly called, visions an agreement between the State (when the majority of its citizens are Catholic) and the Church to help and protect each other in the realization of their respective ends. It sees an effective col-

---

[5] Cf. J. C. Murray, "St. Robert Bellarmine on the Indirect Power," *Theological Studies,* 9 (1948), 491–535.

laboration expressed in positive assistance given in intimate cooperation. Benefits that this system would bring to the Church include the recognition of Catholicism as the State Church, the exclusive reservation of public office to those practicing this State religion, diplomatic relations with the Holy See, State support for propagation of religious doctrines, and, finally, State intolerance regarding the propagation of any heretical or pagan religion.[6] This theory is given by certain Catholic authors as a quasi norm which Catholics throughout the world must seek to realize in their respective governments where possible; where it is, as yet, not possible, then Catholics may demand religious freedom from these State governments.

To summarize the moral theory: in principle (thesis), a harmonious union of Church and State is to be preferred and separation is to be rejected. Separation of Church and State is rejected because it is usually rationalistic, denying revelation and all elements of divine positive law (e.g., the existence of the Church). Moreover, in practice, separation of Church and State is incompatible with the true liberty of the Church as a sovereign and independent society. Many Popes, proponents of this view argue, have declared separation to be "impious, irrational and injurious." Yet in fact (hypothesis) separation can be tolerated when Catholics are a minority in any State. The State would then have an absolute and negative obligation not to hinder the Church, and a positive obligation to help the Church. The positive obligation binds only when such help to the Church is not contrary to the common good of the State. The common good, therefore, is the State's primary end; and, if union with the Church endangers the common good, separation can be *tolerated* in any given State.

It is this theory which raises grave fears as to the Catholic Church's role in any given society. It is even argued that as Catholics become numerically stronger in the United States (as bigger birth rates among Catholics seem to indicate), the

[6] This is very similar to the mandate given by Luther to the princes in *An den Christlichen Adel* (Weimar ed., t. VI, p. 408).

evil day will come when Catholics, being the majority, will revise the Constitution to fit the above theory of thesis-hypothesis.

Our purpose is to investigate the meaning of religious freedom and tolerance and then to elucidate the principles that will be helpful in guiding the layman to "think with the Church" in this difficult area. First of all, we shall outline those views on religious freedom which have been advocated by some Catholic theologians of the past and which cause grave concern among our non-Catholic brethren. Then we shall turn to a sketch of the notion of "tolerance" that has developed in non-Catholic circles from the days of the Reformation to the present, with particular attention to the thought of Martin Luther and the leading figures of *Aufklärung* and the contemporary scene. In the course of this historical sketch we shall of necessity have to consider the secularization of Western civilization that has been operative from the later Middle Ages to the present and the one-sided ecclesiology that resulted as a reaction of orthodox theologians to the pressures of that secularization. Finally, in the final portion of our study, we shall inspect the notions of "negative" and "positive" tolerance in the light of Catholic tradition, offering some reflections on the concrete attitude that should characterize the Catholic in a pluralistic society such as ours. Both theoretically and practically, the problem of religious freedom is probably one of the greatest and most important theological questions of our day. A clear understanding of its nature and the thought given to it by eminent Catholic theologians deserves the greatest study. As we have pointed out earlier, the layman must explain and defend the Church in modern society. Thus it would be lamentable if he were not prepared to give authoritative, theological, and philosophical arguments against the all too logical results of the "thesis-hypothesis theory" regarding religious toleration. Indeed, one might almost say that the Church's witness in a world of rapidly expanding internationalism and totalitarianism will either fall or rise according to the answer we give to the problems of religious freedom.[7] No other problem so excites the fears and raises the suspicions of non-Catholics as does this one. If the layman is ignorant of the elements of a response, the gravest consequences are in store for any form of lay apostolate.

This theory of "thesis-hypothesis" has disturbed more than one Catholic author, for simple honesty compels us to admit that Protestant fears are indeed not groundless if this theory be interpreted as the official stand of the Church. Moreover, how can this theory be aligned, for example, with the thought expressed by Pope Gregory IX to the French bishops in 1233: "The same kindness must be displayed to Jews by Christians as we want shown to Christians living in pagan lands."[8] The notion of religious toleration expressed by the thesis-hypothesis view makes the Church's witness seem hypocritical and perfidious in an age when whole regimes of totalitarianism are built on similar ideological grounds. Such a theory is injurious to the sacred Catholic tradition of religious freedom. We must, however, admit in all honesty that there is a real division among Catholic theologians on the nature of tolerance, whose meaning we shall investigate in the following pages. In this section we will be concerned first with examining the various meanings of the word "tolerance" in different authors and with an analysis of the various theological, philosophical, and political arguments for advocating religious freedom as a firmly grounded principle or thesis, contrary to the view that it can be granted only as an "hypothesis" or prudential accommodation to circumstances when Catholics do not constitute a political majority. In the second place we shall consider the Church's attitude toward tolerance as reflected in pontifical documents and the councils of the Church. Here we shall present the principles of religious freedom which constitute the working tools of achieving respect for truth and the worth of the individual person.

[7] C. Santamaria, "l'Eglise et les libertés dans l'histoire," l'Eglise et la Liberté (Paris, 1952), pp. 225–226.
[8] "Est autem judaeis a Christianis exhibenda benignitas, quam Christianis in paganismo existentibus cupimus exhiberi."

CHAPTER VII

BACKGROUND OF THE NOTION OF TOLERANCE

THE history of toleration is a long and a complicated one, and we have no wish to investigate it completely here. This work has been partly fulfilled in the monumental study of J. Lecler, *Toleration and the Reformation*,[1] which traces this notion from the Bible through the end of the sixteenth century.

For practical purposes the modern notion of toleration dates from the time of the *Aufklärung* in Europe, with its rationalistic approach to religion and the history of religions. Our principal aim in this section is to give a general background for understanding both the modern and the Catholic meaning of tolerance.

For some strange reason, a great number of European and American Protestants have the notion that the modern emphasis on religious liberty and toleration has its roots in the Protestant Reformation. It was Luther, they claim, who first overthrew the tyrant of Rome and loudly proclaimed the idea of the sacredness of human conscience and its freedom vis-à-vis all secular and religious authorities. It is hard to trace the origin of such a myth, for the historical truth of the matter is that Luther and the first reformers were as intolerant as any medieval Church had ever been. In many respects, the early reform was even more severe. The impartial historical work of John Kühn has shown this beyond any shadow of real doubt.[2] Without making

---

[1] New York, Association Press, 1960.
[2] *Toleranz und Offenbarung* (Leipzig, 1923), pp. 100–126.

122

the necessary distinction between objective truth and an erroneous conscience (which the medieval theologians had worked out to great satisfaction), Luther simply made Scripture the objective and absolute norm of tolerance. It might be added, by way of anticipation, that it was his own interpretation of Scripture which became the ultimate norm. *Est mihi revelatum*, he will claim at Augsburg. Conscience is obliged in an absolute manner by the religious truth contained in the New Testament and as interpreted by Martin Luther. We will see how this notion slowly led Luther to a form of intolerance unheard of in the Church of the pre-Reformation period. Let us investigate this period more closely.[3]

The issues leading to the Protestant revolt culminated in the fixing of the famous 95 theses to the church door of Wittenberg in 1517 by the young priest, Martin Luther. The notion of created grace, indulgences, justification by faith, the uselessness of works, and the consequent notion of merit were all part of his system. Although we cannot, within the confines of our study, delve deeply into the theological background of the Reformation,[4] we can note that for Luther the main strength of the Reformation comes from the fact that man has been gratuitously and undeservingly saved by the grace of God. In this first and principal justification, man does absolutely nothing. Man passively receives this justification from Christ in utter confidence and trust that God will cover his sins and no longer impute them to himself. The Christian is free solely in that he must renounce the vain effort to become sinless, consent to God's mercy, and allow God's saving action to forgive him.[5]

---

[3] For other works consulted, see J. Kühn, op. cit., pp. 72–139. N. Paulus, *Protestantismus und toleranz im 16 Jahrhundert* (Freiburg, 1911), pp. 20–65; H. Hermelink, *Der Toleranz Begriff im Reformations Zeitalter* (Leipzig, 1908); R. Bainton, "The Development and Consistency of Luther's Attitude to Religious Liberty," *Harvard Theological Review*, 15 (1939), 107–149.

[4] For general background both theological and sociological to this period, see F. Loofs, *Leitfaden zur Dogmengeschichte* (Berlin, 1924), pp. 696–724; E. De Moreau, *La Crise religieuse du XVIe Siècle*, I (Paris, 1950); H. Rondet, *Gratia Christi* (Paris, 1948), pp. 259–272.

[5] *In Rom* (ed. Ficter, II, 180, 332 et pass.).

There is little meaning to human freedom in this process of justification, since man remains totally corrupt, even after extrinsic justification has taken place. In the *De Servo Arbitrio*, Luther so emphasizes the sovereignty of God that God does with His creature whatever He wants. In God's hands, man is a pure instrument: "Thus the human will is like a rider on a horse where the person goes whithersoever God wishes, as the psalmist says: I am become a beast and am always with thee. If the person is controlled by Satan, it is Satan who directs whithersover he wills man to go."[6] In any case, the Christian is free from all works and the law. "Faith is enough for the Christian. He does not need any works; he is definitely freed from all commandments and all laws and if he is free from them, he is surely free. Such is Christian liberty, and faith alone causes it."[7] It is clear that in such a context there is no longer any need for a visible Church. The only role for visible realities lies in the conferring of baptism and the preaching of the Gospel.[8]

Thus, at the beginning of the Reformation period, Luther advocated a rather liberal view as regards tolerance. It should be noted, however, that many of Luther's early pronouncements were intended to persuade Catholic rulers to mitigate their own struggle against the incipient reform: "I proclaim and loudly proclaim: laws, whether they come from men or angels, cannot be imposed on Christians without their consent, for they are free with regard to all things."[9] Yet, even in this early period there were foreshadowings of the restrictions which Luther was later to impose in very strong language. "Conscience should not be bound in anything except the word of God."[10] Thus as early as 1525 when he wrote his *De Servo Arbitrio*, Luther began to limit the free exercise of conscience which he had loudly proclaimed at the beginning of his reform.

---

[6] *De Servo Arbitrio* (ed. Clemen., III, p. 126).
[7] Cf. *Werke* (cited after this as W.), t. VII, p. 55.
[8] *Von dem Pabsttum zu Rom* (W., t. VI, pp. 292–300).
[9] W., t. VI, p. 537.
[10] W., t. XVIII, p. 624.

It would be a grave injustice, moreover, to say that Luther advocated a relativistic type of tolerance based on the presupposition that doctrines are meaningless. This type of tolerance is a product of the rationalism of the eighteenth and nineteenth centuries. Luther cursed the charity which would make light of doctrine or belief. Scripture was the ultimate source of all authority and the ultimate objective former of every correct conscience. This was so true for Luther that he allowed no freedom for an erroneous conscience, for everyone who differed from him with regard to Scripture was in objective error. Luther infallibly interpreted Scripture. "If our theology achieves certainty, it is because it takes us away from ourselves and puts us outside ourselves so that we no longer rely on our own strength, our conscience, our sense, our personality, our works, but only what is beyond ourselves, namely the promise and truth of God who cannot deceive us."[11]

Nevertheless, during the first years of the reform Luther advocated a toleration firmly opposed to the use of any type of violence. He based his stand on the fact that faith, by its very definition, cannot be forced; for it is essentially a free action.[12] Faith cannot be generated by force, but results from the divine action of the Spirit. "The civil authority should not prevent anyone from teaching and believing what he likes, be it the gospel or falsehood."[13]

Luther's policy remained essentially unchanged even after some fanatics at Wittenberg, basing themselves on Scripture, violently opposed his dogmatic views. Even the Anabaptists, who wished to weed out the Eschatological Kingdom of the saved here below, were to be given toleration. This was in 1524.[14]

Yet, after 1524, some type of external organization and regulation had to be given to the reform. In elaborating this organization Luther was gradually led to take on a progressively more intolerant attitude toward those who differed from him. In the last analysis, those who opposed Luther opposed God Himself.

[11] W., t. XL, I, p. 589. [13] W., t. XVIII, p. 209.
[12] W., t. XI, p. 264. [14] W., t. VIII, pp. 676–688; XV, pp. 218–219.

The reformer then made an appeal to the secular authorities to enforce his interpretation of Scripture and to help propagate the new doctrines. We see the beginnings of this in his *Addresses to the Christian Nobles*.[15] In these, Luther grants three main intolerant mandates to the secular authority: it would have the power to help preach the Gospel; it would have the power to prevent the teaching of false and heretical doctrines in the kingdom; it must see to it that all come to hear the word of God, compelling them to do so if necessary.[16] It is true that no one could be compelled to believe, but men could be compelled to come to hear the sermons of the Gospel: "Our princes do not impose the faith and the gospel, but they repress outward abominations. Since the canons themselves acknowledge the princes' rights in outward matters, they stand self-condemned. The princes should indeed suppress public crime, perjury and patent blasphemy of God's name, but in this they do not compel the person in any way to believe or not to believe."[17]

Luther's ultimate conclusion in regard to public peace and tolerance in the community was the famous dictum: *Cuius regio, illius religio.* Luther was forced into this position by strife and struggles in various parts of the empire. To a group who appealed to their consciences in order to hear Mass, Luther answered: "This does not help them, for they should first be required to prove their good conscience by the Scriptures or by accepting instruction . . . [since they refuse this] they bear clear witness against themselves that they have made up their own kind of conscience and that this is but a conscience in appearance. A really good conscience desires nothing more than to listen to the teachings of the Scriptures and to examine itself with the help of the Scriptures."[18] The problem of the erroneous conscience — so laboriously worked out by the later Scholastics — is given short shrift and dismissed. The ultimate norm of tolerance is not what is consciously recognized by a

[15] W., t. VI, p. 408.

[16] J. Kühn, *op. cit.*, p. 101 ff.

[17] W. *Briefe*, t. III, p. 616.

[18] W. *Briefe*, t. IV, p. 28.

particular person as true or false, but rather the teachings of Scripture, of which Luther believes himself the infallible guide. In 1529, Luther openly gave the civil princes the power to compel people to listen to the preaching of the Gospel: "Even if people do not believe, they should be driven to the sermon because of the Ten Commandments, in order to learn at least the outward works of obedience."[19]

This intolerance goes so far as to propose death for those who refuse or for those who advocate doctrines which are "frankly blasphemous." This is indeed a very strange phrase from the champion of religious tolerance. In the last analysis, it is Luther or the reformers who must determine what is "frankly blasphemous." We must listen to the words of Melanchthon when he says: "My opinion is that those who proclaim tenets that are frankly blasphemous, even if they are not rebels, should be done to death by the civil authorities."[20] Luther concurred in this judgment, for he said in 1530: "But there are other heretics who dare teach matters contrary to the faith as it is clearly founded on the Scriptures and professed by all of Christendom . . . these heretics presume to teach among other things that Christ is not God, but only man. . . . Such people should not be tolerated but punished as public blasphemers. Moses lays down in his law that such blasphemers, and all false teachers, should be stoned."[21] This will be the general intolerant attitude he takes against the Anabaptists[22] and in general against all who differ with him on matters which he considered to be fundamental to Christianity. When others claimed the same right as he in interpreting Scripture, he set himself up as the standard of truth, refusing to concede this same right to other groups.

---

[19] W. Briefe, t. V, pp. 136–137; "Cogendi sunt ad Conciones," ibid., V, p. 137.

[20] Epist Melan., lib. 5, n. 664 (Corpus Reformatorum, t. II, c. 18).

[21] W., t. XXXI, I, pp. 208–209.

[22] For a full history of this whole period, see J. Lecler, Toleration and the Reformation, I (New York, 1960), pp. 193–223; E. Troeltsch, The Social Teaching of the Christian Churches (London, 1959), pp. 28–46.

We have dwelt on Luther's policy of toleration at some length in order to show the falsity of the claim that true toleration had its origin with the reform. To a large extent, even well-informed Catholics have too often submitted to such a myth. Whatever the origins of religious tolerance as we know them today (we shall study them in our next section), we must clearly be rid of the false impression that it started with Luther and the reform. Our purpose is not to enter into any sort of anti-Protestant polemic, but simply to discover, with Protestants and with all men of good will, the real philosophical and theological foundation for a true religious respect of conscience, a respect rooted in love. Let us now turn to some of the more basic elements in the evolution toward the modern conception of religious freedom. The real origins must be sought in the *Aufklärung* of the eighteenth and nineteenth centuries.

This period is marked by a series of religious, philosophical, and sociological events. It would be too long a task to investigate the whole process of secularization of public life and institution from the Middle Ages to the late nineteenth century. The *Aufklärung* is simply the result of a series of ecclesiological and political breakdowns from the later Middle Ages.[23] The disruption of Christian unity had a great effect on the development of a rationalistically inspired tolerance. Because of the warring factions of broken Christianity, the rationalists of this period came to the conclusion that no confession has the complete truth. They advocated, consequently, a relativism in matters of dogma. What matters, the rationalists argued, is not what one believes, but that one finally arrives at his goal. What developments in Western civilization caused this attitude to arise? One was undoubtedly the impoverished, shortsighted

---

[23] See the whole development of this in Georges de Lagarde, *La naissance de l'Esprit laique au déclin du Moyen Age* (Louvain, 1952–1956), 5 vols. This work is extremely important in showing the slow separation not only of Church and State, but also of the whole of society from theological influence. This is important in the study of the history of toleration, for such a secularistic approach to life inevitably leads to a relativistic interpretation of all dogmas and truths. The modern mind is filled with this type of tolerance.

ecclesiology of later Scholasticism, still dominant in the eighteenth century and the source of much current concern. Some reactions against this juridically dominated concept of the Church have been excessive and were censured by Pius XII in *Humani Generis*,[24] but many contemporary theologians have made significant contributions to the bases upon which a sound ecclesiology must be built. Of special interest is the work of those who have probed the relationship between Church and State.

The Church-State struggle began as far back as Gregory VIII and its connected problems. Later Scholastics, anxious to defend the Church, began to conceive of this supernatural society as an essentially juridical *societas* with its own rights, in opposition to the *societas civilis*. Although the concept of the Church as a society independent of and distinct from the secular power was an element common to the teaching of such Fathers as Ambrose[25] and Augustine,[26] the notion came into prominence and received its more precise formulation at the hands of the medieval canonists. Thus began the separation of ecclesiology from other theological tracts; it soon became an apologetics.[27] Various movements, in particular those which denied totally the visible character of the Church and put emphasis on its "spiritual" nature, were set in motion by such leaders as Wycliffe and Huss. These tendencies only served to lead theologians to give further emphasis in ecclesiology on the external elements in the Church. If one wishes to have proof of the excessive emphasis given by ecclesiologists of this period to the external features of the Church let him consult one of the greatest theologians of the fifteenth century, Turrecremata. Study his *Summa de ecclesia*, published at Rome in 1489. In Turrecremata and other authors of this period we do not find one word on the interior and spiritual element of the Church! The result, then, of this whole movement was an excessive emphasis on

---

24 *AAS*, 42 (1950), 563.
25 St. Ambrose, *Epist.*, 12, 4 (*P.L.* 16, 1003–1004).
26 St. Augustine, *De Civitate Dei*, 5, 19 (*P.L.* 41, 166).
27 Y. Congar, *The Mystery of the Temple* (Baltimore, 1960), pp. 97–117.

the hierarchical and external aspects of the Church.[28] Even the titles of these ecclesiological writings betray their one-sided emphasis. We find, for example, "On the Christian Rule" by James of Viterbo (1301), "On the Royal and Papal Power" by Giles of Rome (1301), "On the Power of the Pope" by H. Noel (1309), etc.

The earlier errors of Huss and Wycliffe, coupled with a need of true reform in the Church *in capite et in membris*, led to the sixteenth-century Reformation. Any history of this period of the Church clearly shows that the external is relegated to the secondary and nonessential. Indeed for the Reformers the external was sinfulness. The ecclesiological elaborations since this period have been dominated by bitter polemics between Catholics and Protestants on this issue. Abundant evidence of this can be found in such eminent ecclesiologists as Stapleton (1598) and Bellarmine (1621). After this period, ecclesiology takes on a strictly apologetical point of view in defense of the hierarchy, clergy, sacraments, etc. — in short, the visible aspect of the Church. It became, in the words of Congar, a true "hierarchiology"[29] instead of a total ecclesiology.

Starting in this same period, we have further errors which only served to harden the above tendency: Gallicanism, Jansenism, Febronianism, Josephism, and finally, in Germany, Episcopalianism. All these movements agreed in denying the visible nature of the Church as a society of human beings, many of them sinners and sinful, hierarchically ordered under the successor of St. Peter. The only way to combat them was to stress the outward signs of the Church making it a recognizable society of the faithful, endowed with a divinely constituted magisterium.

As a result of all this, ecclesiologists tended to define the Church as being not only a spiritual institution but also a

---

[28] For abundant bibliography cf. S. Jáki, *Les tendances nouvelles de l'ecclésiologie*, pp. 5–17; Congar, "Affirmations de l'Autorité," in Nedoncelle, *op. cit.*, pp. 76–98.

[29] Y. Congar, "Affirmations de l'Autorité," *op. cit.*, p. 113.

society, properly speaking, visible, institutionally unequal and hierarchical, independent, having its own spiritual finality, with authority on earth to judge in a visible and binding way. The authority of the bishops and, above all, the divinely instituted authority of the Sovereign Pontiff, vicar of Jesus Christ, was heavily emphasized throughout this period.

The scandal of a divided Church led, finally, to dogmatic relativism; the defensive attitude in the Church could not recognize and distinguish what was really of value in the teaching of the *Aufklärung*, namely, that respect for a religiously formed conscience was a good as such. The rationalism of the eighteenth century clearly and validly argued that religion should not lead to war and to slaughter. The rationalists argued that religious sects cannot teach the truth, or at least do not have the fullness of truth because injustices flowed from religious differences. This was the fallacious argument of Voltaire in his work, *A l'Auteur du livre des trois Imposteurs*. There must, consequently, be an arbiter over and above particular religions to judge their worth and validity. This arbiter must be reason, since it alone can know clear and distinct ideas. Anything that is above reason is absurd and ridiculous, and all that conforms with reason is good and valid. Thus a reality such as a properly supernatural order is a contradiction in terms.

Another factor which contributed greatly to the notion of a relativistic tolerance was the discovery of peoples and mentalities unknown up to this time in Europe. Many saw the similarities, for example, between the high moral codes of Buddhism or Confucianism and Christianity and came to the conclusion that Christianity was not an exclusive religion. These religions had values similar to those of Christianity, and this tended to strengthen the notion that both Christianity and various pagan religions were the result of the "religious experience" of some great mystic. Hence, all positive religions reflected the divine order as such and no one religion could claim to rise above the others and assert that it, and it alone, was the exclusively true religion.

All of these factors are more or less responsible for the modern notion of tolerance, which is based on the supposition that religious truths are relative. It is this type of tolerance — as we shall see later — which was and continues to be the object of the Church's direct condemnations. The *Aufklärung* succeeded in evacuating all notions of the transcendent and mysterious in the Christian religion. In the later eighteenth century, Kant was to put the finishing touches on this whole trend. In his system, reason itself gives way to a moral imperative, with the result that not only is reason depreciated, but any possibility of knowledge of God by human reason is an absurdity. This in turn led to Kantian "dogmatism," a word of only one meaning for the modern mind: a blind acceptance of a truth which can never be justified by reason. This, then, is a great source of confusion for the modern mind when the Catholic speaks of "dogma" or "dogmatic intolerance." In the Christian meaning of the term, dogma simply means a truth which God has made known to us and which each man must accept as a personal invitation in faith and response. It is not a blind, unjustified process, but an intensely personal act of self-engagement and dedication to the person of God who reveals Himself by means of this symbol, formula, or dogma.[30] It is personally justified in the very act of faith, for this act is basically an adherence to God who reveals Himself to men in an imperfect but real way. It is totally different from Kant's "dogmatism." Christians ought to avoid the term "dogmatic intolerance" because of this confusion in the meaning of terms. What ought to be emphasized is the refusal to admit any relativism of religious truth in the sense explained above. We will return to this point later.

The nineteenth century was also one of the new discoveries

---

[30] J. Mouroux, *I Believe* (New York, 1959), pp. 13–37; for the texts of the personal structure of the act of faith see the texts of St. Thomas, *Summa Theologiae*, II–II, q. 1, a. 7; III, q. 3, a. 3, ad 1; *De Veritate*, XIV, 8, ad 3; III *In Sent.*, d. 25, q. 1, sol. 1, ad 4. Cf. the famous phrase of St. Thomas: "*Actus credentis non terminatur ad enuntiabile, sed ad rem*" (*Summa Theologiae*, II–II, q. 1, a. 2, ad 2).

in the positive sciences. Rapid strides were made. Soon, however, rationalistically minded critics tried to use the method valid in verifying scientific hypotheses as a general norm of truth. By misusing science in this way, they sought to discredit religious truths. They argued that religious knowledge had been the subject of controversy and strife from the beginning of time and claimed that it would always be so because it was not capable of empirical proof. What is not verifiable or controllable (and religious knowledge can never be totally so), they argued, is either simply false or unattainable by human reason. Religious knowledge is, therefore, simply of a conjectural, imperfect, and relative nature with no possible objective verification. The only practical solution is to consider all religious knowledge as essentially defective and imperfect. Tolerance for these men meant that the diverse interpretations of religions are but symbols or imperfect representations of their object, who is God. Consequently, one set of symbols or religious truths can never totally exclude the truth of another set, and we are thus in the realm of the totally relativistic. All our knowledge of religion is shaped by historicism. Shaped by time, religious truth can evolve into diverse formulas without suffering any deterioration.

Let us examine the charge that religious symbol is a continuously evolving thing. The argument is that all human knowledge must attain God by means of symbols and representations, since man is finite and God belongs to the infinite order. Since these symbols are essentially imperfect and inadequate, we can never attain God as He is objectively. All religious knowledge, therefore, no matter from what religion it comes, is partially true and partially false. A religion — any religion — can never be absolute or exclusive.

The argument has a great amount of truth in it. Its conclusions, however, are too large for its premises. First, we must say that the knowledge we have of God is a true knowledge under pain of talking pure nonsense. If we can have no true and valid human knowledge, then the problem is radically solved and we must be condemned to remain in a perpetual intellectual prison. This knowledge for the Christian comes to him in a double fashion: from nature, i.e., from the things which are created, and from revelation. Since God has created all things, the very things which He has created must tell us something of the person who created, much like the sculpture tells us something of the artist who made it.[31] Then we have the knowledge given to us by revelation. This is personally given to the Christian in and through the person of Jesus Christ who communicates God to men.

Yet all this knowledge we have of God is essentially limited. It can never be perfect, that is, exhaustive, for the simple reason that God is the "other" (although not totally other)[32] and the infinite. Christianity has never professed, nor could it, to have an exhaustive knowledge of God. When theologians speak of the truths of the Christian religion, they mean an imperfect but real knowledge of God as He is in Himself. If this be true, then there is a nucleus of truth in the formulas of faith. These can never change for the simple reason that the true insights they give have been guaranteed by the infallible God. What is true is eternal and can never vary, neither for God nor for men. Yet, this knowledge is not exhaustive. Catholic theology has commonly expressed this imperfection of our knowledge of God by calling it analogical.[33] Indeed, for St. Thomas our knowledge of God is mostly negative. We know what He is not rather than what He is. Nevertheless, the formulas of faith give us a true but imperfect knowledge of God as He really is.

---

[31] This is the metaphysical argument known from the days of Plato and Aristotle. Cf. F. Van Steenberghen, *Ontology* (New York, 1955), pp. 165–180.

[32] I do not wish here to enter into the special problem of our knowledge of God in the theology of Karl Barth. Suffice it to say that he concedes that we can have a true and real knowledge of God in Christ which can never change. Cf. J. Hammer, *Karl Barth* (Westminster, 1962), pp. 6–8; H. Bouillard, *Karl Barth*, I (Paris, 1957), pp. 134–151.

[33] G. P. Klubertanz, *St. Thomas Aquinas on Analogy* (Chicago, 1960), pp. 111–155, along with the appropriate texts of St. Thomas on the subject of analogy.

The other argument which is usually given for disproving the claim of the exclusiveness of the Christian religion is one we have already partially seen — a knowledge of comparative religions. Many religions other than Christianity teach some of the same basic truths concerning certain moral and religious teachings. Here, one may mention the high morality of Confucianism, the monogamy of certain tribes, etc. Since they teach some of the same religious truths as Christianity, the argument goes, this latter religion can no longer claim to be exclusive. As a matter of fact, the truths found in all religions stem from the fact that they are based on similar religious experiences by certain holy and exemplary men who communicate this experience to their followers. The conclusion is simple: there is an equality of all religions since all express the same truths but in different ways. Thus the five great religions are like five fingers on the same hand. None have a permanent and absolute value but all have partial elements of the truth. Relativism in matters religious is now complete and universal.

CHAPTER VIII

TOLERANCE AND THE CHURCH

IT SHOULD be very evident to any Christian and more so to any Catholic that tolerance based on dogmatic indifferentism is to be completely rejected. As we have already seen, the Christian profession of faith is based on truth, and truth as such is not subject to any kind of radical change. The Christian believes that God has spoken to him in a very real way. Because of this, to advocate dogmatic indifference of any kind would be not only a negation of the truth but also and especially treason to the very person of God who has revealed Himself, for He can neither "deceive nor be deceived."[1] Because of this conviction modern existentialists accuse the Catholic as a narrow-minded bigot who holds all others in error and subject to persecution for their false beliefs. Karl Jaspers,[2] a modern existential philosopher, holds that the only absolute truth is to be found in science which bases its conclusions on particulars. In philosophical knowledge, God is attained, but only indirectly by signs and symbols.[3] In this knowledge, however, we do not possess God as He is but only as present to us through our own individual experience of these symbols and signs. There can be no absolute knowledge of God for all, only a series of particular

---

[1] Cf. the Constitution *de Fide Catholica* of the First Vatican Council, Denziger-Bannwart, *Enchiridion Symbolorum*, 1789.

[2] For résumé of his thought, see *The Future of Mankind* (Chicago, 1960).

[3] *Ibid.*, p. 974. See also *Ways to Wisdom* (New Haven, 1954), pp. 120–129.

experiences proper to the individual and uncommunicable.[4] This knowledge has only a personal value. Each man experiences contact with the transcendental in his own way. The world is a symbol which directs each one of us toward God, but each experience is a unique and personal situation which each man has and is.[5] Consequently, the Catholic Church, since it claims to have the total truth for all men and for all times, is proud and intolerant. In it, the tendency to power dominates everything else. Therefore, Jaspers is in favor of a positive tolerance: each man lives his relationship with the transcendental in his own unique way.

Yet is the Christian faith with its absolute claim to religious truth really intolerant of other religions? It all depends on how we understand the word "intolerant." For the Christian, his position is very clear and reasonable. He does not presume to judge the interior sentiments of any man, but he must judge the exterior professions of all men. The Christian simply holds that he truly attains some imperfect but real knowledge of God in and by his faith. Two contradictory statements cannot be both true and false at one and the same time. That Christ is God is either true or false. He cannot be "more or less" God or "almost" God. Truth is in the judgment, and when the Christian makes certain judgments on his religious and revealed truths, he believes that he has infallibly attained truth. If any other judgment should proclaim the opposite, he will hold it to be false. This is not intolerance or narrowness of mind but simply fidelity to what one believes to be absolute truth as given to him by God in faith. To deny this would be equivalent to destroying Christian faith. Such an attitude can never be compatible with Christian faith. Consequently, every semblance of dogmatic indifferentism and relativism must be unequivocally rejected. The Christian's tolerance of others can never be based on any kind of relativism,

---

[4] *The Future of Mankind*, p. 677. See also his *Einfrührung in die Philosophie* (München, 1957), pp. 30–52.
[5] *The Future of Mankind*, p. 83.

whether it come from the rationalism of the modern period or contemporary existentialism.[6] The Christian simply cannot admit any teaching that contradicts the truths of Christianity.

Moreover, to do so would be to betray God who has revealed these truths to the Christian. Christian truths and mysteries are not the work of man nor are they the developments of a religious experience or evolution. They are strictly the Opus Dei, the work of God communicated to men. The Modernists in the beginning of our century taught that Christian truths were evolutions from man's psychological profundity and religious need. These doctrines were condemned without mercy by the Church and rightfully so. To admit this interpretation of Catholic dogma is to empty Christianity of all its properly supernatural content. When God speaks, man must only listen and obey, and once man has heard, he has no alternative but acceptance, yet man must listen in an intimately personal response of faith. Faith is that gift of God which elevates us to see all things as God sees them; nevertheless, man must cooperate. The Council of Trent made this very clear:

> . . . the Holy Council declares that in the case of adults justification must begin with God's prevenient grace through Jesus Christ. That is, it must begin with God's call, a call which they do not merit. The purpose of this call is that they who are turned away from God by sin may, awakened and assisted by His grace, be disposed to turn to their own justification by freely assenting to and co-operating with that grace. The result is that when God touches the heart of man with the illumination of the Holy Spirit, the man who accepts that inspiration certainly does something, since he could reject it; on the other hand, by his own free will, without God's grace he could not take one step toward justice in God's sight.[7]

One is truly free only when one possesses the truth without any fear of error. Modern notions of freedom have tended to

---

[6] For a more detailed analysis of the relationship between the absolute and the relative in modern existential thinking, see the valuable work of W. A. Luijpen, Existential Phenomenology (Pittsburgh, 1960), pp. 260–335.

[7] Denziger-Bannwart, op. cit., 797.

emphasize the aspect of freedom from external constraints; they have not given proper heed to what is essential in freedom, i.e., its internal aspect or freedom from the slavery of illusion and error. Truth and freedom are not opposed; they form one intimate whole, for freedom exists for truth and not vice versa. Our life of freedom develops similarly to our intellectual life. Human freedom is not a pure creative spontaneity. Far from having the magnificence of an unlimited perfection, freedom arises in us as an exigency and appeal, a power of spiritualization and liberation, which is continually exposed to obstacles and is a value to be acquired by conquest. "You shall know the truth and the truth shall make you free." To consider freedom as an end and not as a means to truth is to spell destruction for the human personality. The absolute guarantee of truth in Christianity is the absolute veracity of God addressed to all in and through Christ, who reveals God to men through His Church. What God wants and says is absolutely normative for all men, and for no other reason than that God, the Absolute Truth, has said so. He has spoken to the Christian in Christ. In his attitude to all things, including those who do not agree with him on the truth of his beliefs, the Christian must start from this vantage point. Such is Christian truth. Truth is what the Christian chooses and he chooses it because he is convinced of its truthfulness. His conviction arises from the fact that the Christian has seen, through faith, the complete and absolute truth of Christianity. In addition, the Christian knows that God wills that others embrace the Catholic faith because it is true. In principle, there is nothing arbitrary about truth even though, de facto, this truth is not recognized by all. This truth is neither narrowness of mind, dogmatism, nor fanaticism but an authentic global vision of all things in Christ. It is not "death of mind" to touch the infinite; on the contrary, this contact opens before men's eyes infinite vistas. The truths of faith can never be exhausted by any one man, thought, or particular culture. To give oneself to the infinite who is God is to avoid being closed up in ourselves and our thoughts. Christian exclusivism is founded directly on the real fact that in Christ and Christianity God has spoken and saved man. The ridding of error in religious truth is not a way to death but to life. The oneness of faith is not a death, but a birth of a true diversity which comes from diverse peoples and cultures and temperaments, exercising and living this unique faith in its infinite capabilities in their own way, nourished by it and reflecting upon it with their own native genius. The infinite word of God is inexhaustible for men. There can only be a continuous progression in depth in its realization through the centuries.

One final observation is in order before we leave this section on the history of tolerance and the acceptance of this idea by the Church. We have said that the Church, and she alone, has the essential deposit of faith which is necessary for salvation. The present-day ecumenical movement is an effort by many Christian Churches separated from Rome to find the one true Church of Christ which as yet, they hold, does not exist.[8] The Church holds that, on the contrary, the one, true Church already does exist in the form of the one, Apostolic, Catholic, and Roman Church. Does this lead to the conclusion that all outside of her fold are doomed to perdition? Such a doctrine has never been taught by the Catholic Church, and it has been her constant tradition that unbelievers and Christians actually outside of her visible fold can be saved.[9] We do not propose to show how this can be so: the works on this subject are numerous.[10] A recent letter from the Holy Office on the interpretation of the famous phrase "outside the Church, there is no salvation" made the matter very clear.

Throughout history the Church has always affirmed this truth. The Church can never be accused of any sort of intolerance in this respect. For example, one of the condemned propositions of the Jansenists goes as follows: "It is Semi-

---

[8] G. Thils, *La Théologie Oecumenique* (Louvain, 1960), pp. 10–16.

[9] For a general conspectus, see J. C. Fenton, *The Catholic Church and Salvation* (Westminster, Md., 1958).

[10] It suffices to point out one of the best summaries in the English language, that of R. Lombardi, *The Salvation of the Unbeliever* (London, 1956).

Pelagian to say that Christ died and spilled His blood for all men."[11] This proposition is condemned as false, temerarious, scandalous, and heretical if one means by this statement that Christ died only for the predestined. Catholic doctrine, on the other hand, teaches that Christ died for all men and not simply for the predestined. This truth was explicitly taught by the Church from the time of the local councils of Valence and Quiercy in the ninth century, and has been reaffirmed in our own day.

For over a hundred years the Jansenists caused the Church much trouble. Many of their doctrines strangely resemble those of Father Feeney in Boston. "Christ gave Himself," so the Jansenists said, "for us as an offering to God, not for the elect alone but for all the faithful and for them alone."[12] This doctrine of later Jansenists would seem to be more Catholic than the doctrine of their leader, which had been previously condemned, but it was still rejected as such by the Church since it restrains the absolute universal salvific will of God, including under it only the faithful. God wills the salvation of all men. This is certain Catholic doctrine. We have almost the same doctrine in the following proposition, but with this slight difference: in some way even the pagans must be saved by Christ. When the Jansenists affirmed that "pagans, jews, heretics, and others of this kind in no way receive the influence of Jesus Christ," they were condemned by Pope Alexander VIII. Thus did the Church condemn the narrow exclusion of nonbelievers from salvation.[13]

The salvation of the nonbeliever is a very difficult question to solve. No one doubts that they can be saved. Such a doctrine shocked the Jansenists, yet the Church clung rigidly to its teaching that pagans can be saved. Yet how? Even theologians today discuss the exact "how" of this and full freedom is

---

[11] D.B., 1096.

[12] D.B., 1294: "Christus dedit semetipsum pro nobis oblationem Deo, non pro solis electis, sed pro omnibus et solis fidelibus."

[13] D.B., 1295. For a commentary on this, see X. M. LeBrachelet, "Alexandre VIII," *D.T.C.*, I, C. 751–758. Cf. also D.B., 1291–1321.

allowed them in their discussions. Pagans and nonbelievers must also be saved in some way, yet salvation comes to them by and through the Church. This is not a new doctrine, for the ancient Fathers had taught that *"Extra Ecclesiam nulla salus."* As Pius IX said:

> those who are in invincible ignorance with regard to our holy religion, but who faithfully observe the precepts of the natural law written in their hearts by God and who, obeying God, lead an honest and upright life, can, by divine light and the help of grace, obtain eternal life; for God penetrates, searches and knows the hearts, the spirits, the thoughts and conduct of these men. In His goodness and supreme mercy, He will never consent to punish with eternal pain a man who is not capable of an eternal fault.[14]

With these general observations, we may now proceed to the more positive study of the grounds on which a true Catholic conception of tolerance can be based.

---

[14] Cf. encyclical, *Quanto Conficiamur Moerore*, D.B., 1677.

CHAPTER IX

PRINCIPLES OF TOLERANCE

Introduction

IN THE previous chapter we have seen what tolerance in general is not. Such a procedure is valuable in any study, since it rules out any false perspectives which could easily develop in a study as delicate as that of tolerance. Yet this negative consideration is only an introduction: it is a preparation for the positive exposition in which the basic theological, philosophical, and sociological reasons are given for the idea of tolerance in any society. This positive study will demand many nuances and distinctions. We must be absolute when it comes to the truths of faith, for to sacrifice them to "tolerance" would be to reject the very notion of truth and to turn our backs on God who has revealed these truths to us. It would, moreover, lead only to a pseudo tolerance, an attitude embraced for pragmatic, emotive reasons, not one rooted in convictions. Therefore, truth must necessarily occupy an essential dimension in any discussion of toleration. Yet, in Christianity, this intransigence in and toward truth must always be given, exposed, and received in agapé, love. Truth may never be sacrificed for charity; for such charity would indeed be a mockery, as Luther saw so long ago. "*Maledicta sit caritas quae servatur cum iactura doctrinae fidei*" (Cursed be the charity which is kept at the sacrifice of Christian doctrine).[1] We have already seen the

---

[1] *Commentarium in Ep. ad Gal.*, 5, 9.

false notion of tolerance advocated by doctrinaire liberalism and relativism in past centuries, a concept which still enjoys a great popularity in the modern world. The loyal Catholic can never base his idea of tolerance on the shifting sands of indifferentism or relativism. His notion of tolerance must correspond to the objective truth given to him in and through the Church. His tolerance must be given in truth and in charity.

Our purpose is first to expose in a general way what both negative and positive tolerance can and must mean for the Catholic. By negative tolerance, we simply mean that we may never force others to embrace the faith against their will. By positive tolerance we mean the practice of these virtues which can help us to live in true peace and charity with those who differ from us in their conception of religious faith. After examining these elements of the idea of tolerance we will investigate various theological and philosophical reasons why this idea should be accepted by all Catholics.

1. *Negative Tolerance*

Most Catholic theologians agree with P. Cappello that negative tolerance is a negative permission of evil.[2] We permit or allow an evil to continue because the struggle to eradicate it would cause an even greater evil. Such permission implies at least interior reprobation. The evil permitted is the erroneous religious teaching of non-Catholic faiths. We must reject these teachings, even while allowing them to exist. Our rejection of them is simply an expression of the strict Catholic teaching that the fullness of divine truth is to be found only in the Catholic Church. And to the degree that other religious doctrines are opposed to hers, they are simply false. Tolerance, then, is not and cannot be a virtue properly speaking. The sincere Catholic (as well as every other man who is sincerely convinced of the objective truth of his faith) must strongly desire that all will come to the fullness of truth which is to be found only in the

---

[2] *Summa Juris Publici Ecclesiastici* (Rome, 1928), p. 24. Also in A. Vermeersch, *Tolerance* (New York, 1912), pp. 1–6.

Church, that all will become Catholic so as to enter into the fullness of this divine faith. He can never applaud the objective doctrines of other religions if they contradict his own, and he must lament the fact that religious disunity and divergence really exist.[3] To argue in any other way — be the person a sincere Catholic or Protestant — is to fall into the baneful error of confusing truth with falsehood and relativism, and indifference with tolerance.

Tolerance as such can never be a virtue, but, as we shall see in our exposition of positive tolerance, it is an appeal to other basic Christian virtues, such as respect for the sincerity and conscience of others. From a negative point of view, tolerance looks toward the existence of an *objective* evil, and thus we cannot speak, as do many moderns, of the great virtue of tolerance which is the fruit of modern understanding and society. What most of these men really mean is that religious truths are unimportant, so why quarrel over them. This type of tolerance can never be accepted by any true Catholic or by anyone who respects the truth.

But negative tolerance is not limited to the interior rejection of erroneous religious teachings. It also involves the permission of this evil and the refusal to force anyone to accept the Catholic faith against his will. Although this is not very likely to happen in our day, there is always the danger that coercion of this nature could be applied in some indirect way. If Catholics — or those of other faiths, for that matter — should succeed in introducing inequities into the social, economic, or political orders, a person might be strongly tempted to abandon his own convictions and embrace a faith in which he did not believe for purely pragmatic reasons. We might object that men should have the courage of their convictions, but experience shows that most men are not heroes and that it is unrealistic to expect heroic virtue from them. When enough external pressure is brought to bear on them, most men will not have

[3] A. Leonard, "Freedom of Faith and Civil Toleration," *Tolerance and the Catholic* (New York, 1955), p. 97.

the courage to resist.[4] There is great danger, then, that in countries where Catholics comprise a majority, they might be tempted to create conditions which would gravely jeopardize the freedom of conscience of non-Catholics. That is why Pius XII wrote in his encyclical *Mystici Corporis Christi*: "Faith, without which no one can be pleasing to God, must be a completely free surrender of the understanding and the will. If therefore a case should ever arise in which someone were forced against his will into professing the Catholic faith — contrary to the constant teaching of this Apostolic See — we should be forced to disassociate ourselves from such use of force, as our duty."[5] Belief, as such, is the interior acceptance of some objective truth assented to on the authority of God. Thus it is inconceivable that anyone could be forced to believe contrary to his own convictions. Nevertheless, external force can be applied to make a dissident's life so difficult that he would be strongly tempted to disregard his conscience and act contrary to it. It is this danger which must be eradicated through a proper understanding of negative tolerance. It should be the strict duty of the State to insure effective freedom of conscience, of propaganda, of worship and of teaching to all of the ideological groups which do not constitute a danger to the general welfare of the State in strict accordance with the requirements of natural law and of natural ethics.[6] Suarez called every direct constraint on unbelievers to accept the faith — even civil subjects in a Catholic State — intrinsically evil. He continued by insisting that indirect constraints must also be shunned by the civil authority in virtue of the conception of

---

[4] We apologize for referring continuously to Catholic or Christian countries only. As we shall see, philosophically, the problem of tolerance is an international problem in respecting the basic rights of man. We are fully aware that the problem of tolerance is much worse in many Mohammedan and Far Eastern countries. This is not to be wondered at, for it is only with Christianity and the Judeo-Christian tradition that the rights of man have taken on a basic meaning.

[5] See also his talk to the Roman Rota, *AAS*, 38 (1946), 391–392.

[6] R. Rouquette, "Le Probleme du pluralisme religieux," *l'Eglise et la Liberté* (Paris, 1952), pp. 215–226.

negative tolerance. Freedom of conscience, which is the ultimate justification for allowing existence to objectively false
religious teachings, is revealed by an analysis and consideration
of the true nature of faith in Christianity. For some Catholic
theologians, it is sufficient to consider the utter transcendence
of faith in order to justify completely religious liberty and
toleration.[7] Direct or indirect imposition of Catholicism by
state laws is alien to the Christian religion. The act of faith in
Christianity is essentially a free act both on the part of God
who calls man and on the part of man who freely responds
and gives himself to God. The act of faith, both in Sacred
Scripture and in the tradition of the Church, is an intimate
relationship between the person of the believer and the person of God; consequently, any attempt to force this act on
anyone is tantamount to the destruction of the act of faith
itself. Of its very essence, faith is the response of the human
person to the personal God and is thus the meeting of two
persons. In the act of faith, the whole man is involved in a
deeply personal relationship with God. As St. Thomas put it:
"Belief depends on the will of the believer; but man's will
needs to be prepared by God through grace, so that it may be
raised to things which are above nature."[8] Thus it is worthwhile to examine in some detail what the act of faith means in
Catholic tradition in order to see why negative tolerance is a
basic requirement of the Catholic.

In Scripture, faith is portrayed for us as a concrete reality
which engages man in the totality of his being.[9] It is not
something simply intellectual, but total. We see the Gospel
of St. John making a personal appeal to men's faith by "signs"
which Christ worked. Christ's miracles or signs are a personal
invitation to the person who sees them to belief.[10] These signs
have as their necessary function not only to display an ex-

---

[7] A. Leonard, op. cit., p. 98.
[8] Summa Theologiae, II–II, q. 6, a. 1, ad 3.
[9] J. Mouroux, I Believe (New York, 1959), pp. 19–35.
[10] Jn 2:11; 4:54; 11:40; 12:41.

traordinary event but to conduct men to the very person of Christ as God's envoy. They are intended to disclose Christ as one worthy of men's personal and supreme confidence, trust, and faith. "To see" a miracle was, in both the Old and New Testaments, to see and contemplate the spiritual power of the one who operates that sign. Yet even this remains in the obscurity of faith which a man must personally see, justify, and accept.[11] A miracle was a personal invitation to man to give himself totally and unreservedly to the person of the Redeemer. That is why St. John insists on this notion of faith. God respects His creature, man, exercising His power of salvation in a way in which man can understand it. The glory of Christ (His divinity) is hidden in the Incarnation and can be revealed only to those with faith; but this faith, according to St. John, is born by a personal contemplation of the signs which Christ worked. Nothing could be more foreign to the mentality and thought of this sacred author than to force one to believe. Christ did not do so. He appealed to men's faith with miracles which men had to "see" with faith and which men had to believe to recognize the divine origin of Him who works the miracles. The dramatic character of the miracles revealed for us in the Gospel of St. John comes from the fact that they became the stumbling block of those who saw and refused to believe. In any case, the whole process of faith in Scripture is of an intimate, personal, and absolutely free nature. Any other conception would be completely foreign to the spirit of the New Testament.

In the texts of Scripture, there are two aspects which are clearly brought out in any act of faith. The first is that faith is a total giving of oneself to God. It is essentially a free act and certainly includes the exercise of human liberty.[12] It is God who is the first to beckon to man to come.[13] Because of

---

[11] A. Decoutroy, "La Conception Johannique de la foi," *Nou. Rév., Théo.*, 81 (1959), 569; see also R. Bultmann, *Faith* (London, 1961), pp. 108–109; C. H. Dodd, *Interpretation of the Fourth Gospel* (Cambridge, 1954).

[12] Jn 6:66.

[13] Mt 25:24; Lk 15:1–32; 18:9–14; 19:10.

God's great love — which He has for us while we are yet sinners — man can approach God.[14] It is not that man loved God first but that God loved man first that man now can correspond to the great love of God. Yet this gift still demands something from man which is all important: faith. The glory or the shame of man is that he can say yes or no to God, for this is precisely what is done in the notion of faith. Although man can do absolutely nothing to merit the grace of faith,[15] he can and must give his personal consent to God's work. Against the Judaizers who claimed that the works of the law were necessary for salvation, St. Paul answers time and again that the only attitude a man can and must take before God's gift of life and love is that of faith.[16] For St. John, the same idea of faith prevails. A new creation or birth has been given to the Christian whereby he can enter the kingdom of heaven.[17] Without this new existence, born of baptism and the Holy Spirit, it is impossible to enter therein. This new birth is given only by faith in the Son of God whom a man has freely chosen and received. The prerequisite of this new birth is that men come to believe in Him whom the Father has sent.[18] Those who become voluntarily blind to Christ are sons of the devil, who was a liar from the beginning.[19] They are even now doomed to death because they have refused to believe in the Son of man.[20] Faith is not the conclusion of a syllogism, but the personal call of God to man and man's personal adherence to God as the first truth. "Everyone who believes assents to someone's words; and thus, in any form of belief, it seems that it is the person to whose words the assent is given, who is of principal importance and, as it were, the end; while the individual truths through which one assents to that person are secondary."[21] God gives us faith

---

[14] Rom 3:9 ff.; 5:12; 9:16; 1 Thess 1:4; 2 Thess 2:16.
[15] Rom 5:6; 3:20.
[16] Phil 1:12–18; 3:18–19; Gal 1:11; Rom 3:20; 5:20; Gal 3:16.
[17] Jn 3:5.
[18] Jn 6:29.
[19] Jn 8:41, 44.
[20] L. Cerfaux, The Four Gospels (Westminster, Md., 1960), pp. 75–85.
[21] St. Thomas, Summa Theologiae, II–II, q. 11, a. 1.

and illuminates us as to the truths of faith; but in so doing, He makes personal appeal to man's will and intellect.

We can distinguish further elements in the notion of faith in the New Testament, and it will become clear that all forms of intolerance are excluded from each of these elements.

First, there is the subjective element of the act of faith which a man must make before he can belong to God. It is, as we have seen, primarily God's work, a grace which comes to man from God Himself. It comes from the absolute initiative of God's love for men, and therefore faith cannot be forced from God. It is totally impossible to replace this initiative and influence by human coercion. To substitute man's influence for God's is to mock God's ways and His liberty; it is to deny the supernatural element and constitution of faith. It would be a perfect act of pride on man's part to do what God alone can do for and in man. Not only is this attitude inefficacious in bringing about its end, it renders extremely poor service to the Church and to others. Any force exerted on religious belief would only prevent others from coming to see the faith's true spiritual appeal and obscure its value as the personal act and invitation by God. "A social order which restricts the right of a certain group of people and makes their lives difficult, and a social order which surpasses free discussion, is not favorable to the spread of truth."[22] To try to force the act of faith is to show irreverence for God and a disregard for the basic rules of human psychology in any appeal to truth.

Second, faith is a man's gift of himself in his totality to the loving God who calls him. Faith is a personal relationship between a human person and God. It is, in short, man's total gift of himself to God in a response of voluntary love. Faith is the first act of man's response to this agapé of God revealed through Christ in the Church. Many things can be forced on man but not the act of faith, for faith implies a complete surrender of the will and intellect to God. St. Augustine put it

[22] J. Leclercq, "Etat Chrétien et liberté dans l'Eglise," Vie Intellectuelle, 43 (1949), 99–106.

very beautifully when he said that many external acts can be forced on a man against his liberty. Even our internal acts can be influenced, as when the devil works on our imagination. But belief can never be forced on us from the outside, for the simple reason that belief is a free gift and pledging of oneself to God.[23]

These reflections on the folly and inanity of external coercion in matters of faith are particularly important in any consideration of the relationship between the visible civil society and the Church. Social life must be organized in such a manner that it is favorable to God's grace and faith; it must also foster human freedom. Only when an atmosphere of freedom from any religious restraint to profess faith exists can true faith flourish. There are obvious limits as regards the common good, and we shall later investigate these; but freedom must be the dominant theme for a true growth in faith. In the words of Cardinal Feltin of Paris:

> Social pressure; spiritual emancipation: which will win? as a man, I cannot tell; as a bishop I am bound to choose. And my choice is freedom. At a higher level than the disputes of the schools and political ideologies, freedom assumes a pastoral dimension. The reason is not exterior and secondary, as if the Church were claiming freedom only to accommodate itself to the taste of the day. Freedom lies at the heart of Christianity, which seen from without might look like a system, but thought and lived from within is a living bond between persons, a religion of the spirit. Faith is the encounter of a free gift and a free acceptance; a call on the part of God and a conscious and submissive response to God's voice. . . . Freedom for the sake of freedom, freedom for the sake of approaching nearer to God, such is the Christian order which is ours to promote.[24]

We must also consider the problem from the point of view of the objective content of faith. As we have already seen, God

---

[23] St. Augustine, *Epist. ad Sextum*, n. 19 (*P.L.* 33, 880). See also *In Evangel. Joann.*, Tract. 3, n. 10 (*P.L.* 35, 1401); *Enchiridion*, c. 107 (*P.L.* 40, 282).

[24] *Christianity and Freedom* (London, 1955), pp. 159–163.

has spoken once and for all through His only-begotten Son.[25] This is valid in truth for all men and for all time; it is the eternal truth who is God who has revealed Himself to men. It is absolute, and God demands its acceptance. This truth has been entrusted to the Church, and objectively all who wish to come to the fullness of divine truth must become members of this Church. The Church has received the command to preach this truth to all men until the end of time: "Going, therefore, teach all nations . . . those who believe shall be saved." This is the mission of Holy Church until the second coming of Christ, and it is accomplished by the preaching and teaching authority. This is an absolute Catholic truth.

Yet does this mean that the Church can use all means, even force, to favor her preaching and to spread faith? To answer this, we must look at the end of the Church's preaching and witness. The end is obviously that all men might believe, that all men might come to the act of faith. She is, as the First Vatican Council described her, a sign elevated among the nations so that they might contemplate the spiritual beauty and truth on which she is founded.[26] And just as Christ did not use force to win over His followers but rather appealed to their freedom, so, too, the means which the Church uses today must be adapted to the spiritual end which she seeks to accomplish. The act of faith — as we have seen — is a free and supernatural act. Consequently, the means employed to bring men to make *that* act of faith must be means such as respect its free and supernatural character. The Church's teaching power must respect the double character of the act of faith. The Church will not lead men to faith by force. Rather the Church's preaching must be an appeal to man's freedom, enriched and strengthened by God's grace. Force has absolutely nothing to do with this appeal.[27] It must be the same means that Christ Himself used in His appeal to the chosen people. He never

---

[25] Heb 1:2–5.
[26] Sessio III, *Constitutio Dogmatica de fide*, D.B., 1794.
[27] L. Sturzo, *Church and State*, II (Notre Dame, Ind., 1962), pp. 526–560.

applied force and He even rebuked Peter for trying to use it. If the Gospel of St. John teaches anything, it is that God appeals to man's freedom to choose Christ who manifested Himself in signs and wonders of work and doctrine. So too the Church must be that "continued sign" which appeals to men's minds and souls by the purity and loftiness of her work and doctrine. This is simply the continuation of that work and doctrine which was Christ's.

It has been ably argued by Catholic theologians that force by the civil power may never be used justly for the propagation of any religious faith. If the two powers are complete in their own spheres (as was stressed by Leo XIII) it becomes very difficult indeed to see on what justification the Church or any religious body may appeal to the secular arm to enforce her own end. The proper end of the civil authority is the common public and temporal good of society. These distinctions of ends have been traditionally taught by all Catholic canonists. If this be true, what possible argument could be forwarded as an exception to this sacred rule? It is commonly said, in answer, that this can be done because the Church although without any direct power over the State, has a superiority in virtue of the dignity of her end. Superior dignity of the Church is indeed granted, but this proves nothing because both ends remain distinct, one secular and the other spiritual. In the words of John C. Murray:

It may be that in a Catholic society heretical propaganda does spiritual harm. Granted: nevertheless this is not the kind of harm that secular government, as the agent of public order, is bound by its office to ward off from its citizens. The protection of her members in the possession of their faith is the task of the Church; it is a spiritual, not a political task. And if the Church is too weak to perform this task successfully, she does not by that fact acquire a juridical right to invoke the coercive strength of secular government. If it be asserted that the temporal power is distinct from the spiritual power, sovereign in a limited order distinct from the spiritual power, it cannot be that the distinctions asserted should suddenly vanish to permit the temporal order to become attached to the Church as her 'secular arm' to minister to needs that are not secular but spiritual.[28]

In any case, experience has shown that when the State forcibly intervenes in favor of the Church, the consequences are not at all good for the Church. There is no need to dwell on this point. Suffice it to note that history records definite interventions by the secular authority in favor of the Church for which a Christian can only feel shame. From an international point of view, the exercise of this policy in one "Catholic" country has adverse effects on the Church as a whole and on the image of the Church which non-Catholics have of her. To the rest of the world she appears insincere and unjust when she applies various civil pressures in one part of the globe, yet claims absolute freedom to propagate her doctrine in other parts of the world. We have seen that the freedom of faith demands freedom from all direct or indirect restraint. Would it not be better to renounce all forms of "favoritism" in the international community in which we live, so that the true Catholic doctrine of the Church might all the more be clear to the world in all of its purity? Only an affirmative reply to this question corresponds with the free character of faith. This shows, moreover, that religious freedom is not to be regarded as a lesser evil, but as an acquired principle in a definitive and permanent way. This principle is not based on some kind of political opportunism which can adapt itself to changing conditions, but rather constitutes the very nucleus of the psychological structure of the act of faith as it appears in the New Testament and in Catholic tradition. It is based firmly in the notion of the dignity of the human person and his liberty to respond to the appeal of God. It also acknowledges the super-

---

[28] "Government Repression of Heresy," *The Proceedings of the Third Annual Meeting of the Catholic Theological Society of America* (Chicago, 1948), pp. 67–70. For other articles of Father Murray see "Freedom of Religion," *Theological Studies*, 6 (1945); "Leo XIII: Two Concepts of Government," *Theological Studies*, 14 (1953), pp. 527–550; "St. Robert Bellarmine on the Indirect Power," *Theological Studies*, 9 (1948), 491–535; "Current Theology on Religious Freedom," *Theological Studies*, 10 (1949), 409–435, etc.

natural transcendence of the act of faith. German Catholics, for example, have publicly urged that we abandon once and for all the political principles leading to reciprocal limitations of religious freedom.[29]

This teaching is not new. It reaches back to such ancient doctors as Lactantius[30] and Tertullian. This latter witness appealed to the common law and particularly to the sacred right to honor God according to one's conscience.[31] Both argued that if a man is forced in any way to the faith, he is not offering himself as God wills. Catholic tradition is so full of examples of the appeal of faith to man's freedom that it would be superfluous to cite all of them here. One could read any *Tractatus de Gratia* and find numerous examples to corroborate this thesis. The whole doctrine on grace is an intimate personal dialogue between the loving God who wishes to give Himself to man and man's free response to this gift. Christian tradition has always stated that man is capable of free determination since he has free will and yet, to reach his supernatural goal which is God's intention, grace is absolutely necessary. In spite of the errors of Pelagius on the nature of grace and free will, St. Augustine defended this doctrine of freedom.[32] The Councils of the Church have continually affirmed that man remains free to choose or not to choose, even though his freedom has been wounded by the original fall.[33] If man sins, it is imputable to himself and to no one else. He can even perform some good works on the natural plane, but of his own free will he cannot in any way merit supernaturally without God's grace. Because of free will, man is capable of sin, but alone he cannot attain the spiritual freedom of a son of God or perform supernaturally

[29] E. Von Kuhnelt-Leddihn, "Katholische Toleranz," *Wort und Wahrheit*, 22 (1949), 353.

[30] *Divin. Instit.*, V, 20 (*P.L.* 6, C. 614–617).

[31] *Ad Scapulam*, II (*P.L.* 1, C. 699). For this whole early period see H. Doerriès, *Constantine and Religious Liberty* (New Haven, 1960), pp. 1–15.

[32] Cf. St. Augustine, *De natura et gratia*, 8 (*P.L.* 44, 251); *De perfectione iustitiae hominis*, 5 (*P.L.* 44, 296); *Enchiridion*, 137 (*P.L.* 40, 282, etc.).

[33] See the Council of Orange, D.B., 174, and the Council of Trent, D.B., 814.

meritorious actions. The capacity to perform such works can only come first through God's grace and, after this, through man's cooperation with that grace. Thus, from the time of St. Augustine, the Church's tradition has always kept a balance between these two truths of faith. Against Godescalc in the ninth century and Luther in the sixteenth, she upheld human liberty; against Pelagius and the Semi-Pelagians of the fifth and sixth centuries she upheld that belief in God in the scriptural sense of the word was principally and initially the *Opus Dei*, the work of God. She has made her own the words of St. Augustine: "Grace is not given to us because of our merits, and no merit precedes grace. . . . It is only when grace has been given that merit begins, but merit only begins, by it. If grace be taken away, man falls and his free will could not lift him up again, since it was his free will which made man fall."[34]

It would be completely out of place to cite the glorious Scholastic tradition on the need for grace and the absolute freedom of the act of faith.[35] It is sufficient to say that St. Thomas' doctrine on grace and faith admirably develops and keeps these traditional truths in Christianity: faith is a pure grace of God which man must receive of his own free will. Once received he can cooperate on this supernaturally elevated plane in what Catholic tradition calls merit. In its fourteenth chapter on the process of justification, the Council of Trent explains what it means by merit.[36] Grace is a reality which inheres in man. Thus there is a vital union between man, grace, and God. It follows that this reality of grace can grow by and through human activity once man is elevated to this supernatural state. This increase in grace is called merit. It is simply the growth of grace within us and it can grow only because we truly share in the life of God. It is therefore God's dynamic action in us in which we freely cooperate. This is simply an explicit formula-

---

[34] De Gratia et Libero Arbitrio, 13 (P.L. 44, 889–890).

[35] For full development, see A. Landgraf, Dogmengeschichte der Frühscholastik I. Die Gnadenlehre, I (Ratisbon, 1952), pp. 200–296.

[36] R. Gleason, Grace (New York, 1962), pp. 212–222.

tion of Catholic tradition with regard to the action of God and man in this process of justification and faith.

We can now come to some general conclusions regarding the Catholic tradition on the act of faith and man's freedom therein. The act of faith is a free orientation of man in his totality to God. Faith, even considered simply as knowledge, is an activity that engages the whole person and not only his intelligence. It is with his whole life and being that man goes to the truth which touches him interiorly. The work, for instance, of Newman shows abundantly well that this is absolutely true in the knowledge of faith. This knowledge touches all of our being since it makes us know of the existence of an entirely new end to human life.

The collaboration of all the psychological forces in man are necessary for the act of faith. This personal and intimate adherence of the believer to God appears even more clear when we stop to consider that the conviction of faith does not lean on any properly intellectual penetration of the mystery, but on the very word of a loving and intelligent being in whom we place our full confidence, trust, and love.[37] At the very basis of the structures of faith, there is a totally free renunciation of our own proper intellectual autonomy, a respectful and loving submission to the Divine Person who addresses Himself to us in that very act of faith. These two ideas of man's freedom and God's gratuitous call are foremost in the Christian tradition. One famous theologian concludes that "the reception of the word of God ought not just to put into action my speculative faculty but also my whole personality and liberty; this is true because it is a question — in the act of faith — of being a listener to *someone* and not to some thing or a thought; we must speak of the 'thou' and not of the 'it'; yet, we formally listen to a person only in the act where one consents freely to such an act, i.e., to give or to refuse one's whole being."[38]

[37] F. Mallet, *Qu'est ce que la Foi?* (Paris, 1946), pp. 5–6.
[38] L. Malevez, "Théologie dialectique," in *Révue de Science Religieuse,* 28 (1938), 387.

Martin Buber has focused attention on the "I-Thou" relationship between the believer and God as an intimately personal contact between two loving personalities.[39] If faith is essentially a free act of the person involved, its objective is also of an extremely personal nature. We believe in God who has given Himself to us in Christ. Yet this faith — if it be true — continuously seeks specific truths which are the formulations of the realities central to this personal world of the "I-Thou." Catholic faith is not the pure confidence of classical Protestantism, but neither is it a pure system of speculative truths whose end would simply enrich us with knowledge of the celestial world. Such an attitude — or attitudes — simply cannot be justified from a scriptural or traditional point of view. The Catholic faith is totally directed to the Gospel, to a message of hope and salvation. The Church in its early tradition as well as in the Scholastic period was unanimous in calling faith the *Substantia rerum sperandarum*. The act of faith consists fundamentally in the affirmation of intimate personal and free relationships between God and man. The Council of Trent, as we have seen, says the same thing when it claims that the first object of the faith of the adult convert is justification effected in him by God through His gratuitous grace.[40] St. Thomas expressed this throughout his works when he said that the essential feature of the act of faith is God Himself personally given supernaturally to man who must freely accept Him. All other truths are only particular expressions of this one central truth.[41] The believer doesn't give his belief simply to a series of particular dogmas, but to a personal God who has lovingly revealed Himself. When the believer wishes to specify and make his individual beliefs more clear, he simply assents to particular truths guaranteed by that loving God. This act is not so much the result of a personal experience as a response to a revelation

---

[39] *I and Thou* (New York, 1937).

[40] Sessio VI, Ch. 6, D.B., 798.

[41] *De Veritate*, XIV, 8, ad 3; *Summa Theologica*, II–II, q. 1, a. 7; III, q. 3, a. 3, ad 1; In 3 *Sent.*, d. 23, 2. 1; d. 25, a. 1, q. 1, sol. 4. *De Caritate* 3, c; *In Joannem*, c. VI, lect. 5, n. 3, etc.

of God to man, accepted because of the authority of this divine revelation and because the believer has "seen" God personally calling to him in the appeal of faith.[42] Since it is an affirmation of the existence of supernatural realities, Christian faith, by its very definition, implies a total change of our human orientations: "In the light of this . . . we can see the force of the old scholastic adage: *credere Deum, credere Deo, credere in Deum.* Believe in God because God is the very object of our faith and everything else is perceived in relation to Him. Believe what God says because He is the motive of our belief in all. Believe unto God because God is our final end towards which we are going and which we constantly seek."[43] Thus, as in the Pauline sense of the word, faith is that intimately personal and firm attachment to the person of Christ, the Lord and Master. It is an intimately personal engagement of man in all that he is and has, since it is in function of a total dynamism of the human spirit which seeks its last end. This is why all of Christian tradition has seen in the act of faith "the beginning of eternal life in us."

Our conclusion is extremely simple. Given this personal and intimate complexus of faith as a dialogue between the human person who responds and the person of God who calls him to this new life and being, any kind of force — either direct or indirect — is nothing short of sacrilege. Any human act is totally incapable of bringing it about, and to attempt in any way to do so is a flagrant violation of the supernatural character of faith, the dignity of the human person, and the totally free initiative and freedom of God Himself.

2. Positive Elements of Tolerance

We have seen in the previous pages the more or less negative elements which should characterize a Catholic's attitude toward tolerance: the rejection of all forms of relativism and indiffer-

---

[42] J. Levie, "Faith and Intellectual Sincerity," *Faith, Reason and the Gospels* (Westminster, Md., 1961), pp. 42–67; M. D'Arcy, *The Nature of Belief* (London, 1931), pp. 24–62.

[43] G. Thils, *Christian Holiness* (Tielt, 1961), p. 375.

ence; and the refusal to apply any civic or restrictive censures
in the acceptance or practice of religious faith. To sum up, the
Catholic can never accept the thesis that liberty of conscience
means freedom to believe or to disbelieve anything one chooses
to believe or disbelieve.[44] All men are bound by objective truth
revealed once and for all through Christ the Savior. In this
sense, a doctrinal error has no objective reality or claim to adherence by anyone. Thus some argue that "error has no rights"
and consequently should not be tolerated. But this is to put
the whole matter in poor perspective. Of course error has no
rights. But persons do, even if they hold objectively erroneous
views. It is a sound teaching of Catholic theology that although
men are bound in the objective order to accept God's revelation as proposed to them by the Church, the formal morality
of any action is to be measured entirely in terms of the dictate
of conscience at the moment this act is performed. Since we
cannot here investigate the evolution of the notion of erroneous
conscience,[45] it is sufficient to say that when a conscience is
honestly formed — whether it correspond to objective truth or
not — it must be followed under penalty of sin. This is the
final position of the great Scholastics of the thirteenth century
as well as that of traditional Catholic theology through the
centuries. In the words of St. Thomas: "We must therefore
hold, without qualification, that whether the reason be correct
or mistaken, the will which is at variance with it is always
evil."[46] This is not to say that the objective norm is not important. St. Thomas and other Catholic theologians have always emphasized that all men have the grave moral obligation
to form their consciences according to God's objective revelation. Yet, because of various circumstances beyond an in-

---

[44] See the remarkable pamphlet by Cardinal Lercaro, *Religious Tolerance in
Catholic Tradition* (The American Press, 1960), pp. 1–9.

[45] For a full treatment of the evolution of erroneous conscience in the
Scholastics as well as in the Church's teaching, see the remarkable book of
E. D'Arcy, *Conscience and its Right to Freedom* (New York, 1961); also
C. A. Pierce, *Conscience in the New Testament* (London, 1958).

[46] As quoted in D' Arcy, *op. cit.*, p. 108.

dividual's control, e.g. birth in another religion, environment, training, he may well be invincibly ignorant of this true objective norm and have formed his conscience in an honest and sincere way according to what is objectively incorrect. In such a case, man's conscience must direct all of his actions under pain of sin since he has no other way of knowing God's commands. In the words of Pius XI: "We are both proud and happy to fight for the freedom of consciences [la libertà delle coscienze], and not, as I was inadvertently led to say, for freedom of conscience [la libertà di coscienza], an ambiguous expression that is all too often wrongly used to mean complete independence of conscience, which is absurd when applied to a soul created and redeemed by God."[47]

In pluralistic societies, as are most countries of the World, whole groups of persons whose consciences have been formed by faiths alien to that of the Catholic are found. Negative tolerance certainly gives Catholics living in such societies some basic and fundamental orientations. Nevertheless, since they must live in intimate contact with their neighbors, these Catholics need a positive attitude toward those who do not share their faith. We have an obligation in conscience to collaborate with them in such fields as health, the common good of the body politic, and the people temporal. This simple requirement is necessary to make social life livable and worthy of man. On what principles and attitudes can we base an active and positive tolerance toward these groups?[48] We have already said that the Catholic truths of faith can never be jeopardized or sacrificed, yet tolerance must be expressed in love. What does this mean?

To formulate a genuinely Christian answer to this question is difficult, requiring much patience and good will. Above all, this answer must respect both truth and charity. It must reflect our profound and unshakable faith in the Word of the revealing God and at the same time must be addressed to our

---

[47] Non abbiamo bisogno, in AAS, 23 (1931), 301–302.
[48] For interesting exchange of various ideas in a pluralistic society, see John Cogley, ed., Religion in America (New York, 1960).

brothers in the spirit of Christian charity. How many times do we confuse the love of objective truth with an affirmation of self over and above the feelings and the considerations of those who, in good faith, do not agree with us? This does not mean that we must deny the truth of what we believe; this would be infidelity to the truth, to ourselves, and to God. But there are many ways to cooperate in common goals within the confines of the truths which we do hold in common.

There are ways of preaching the truths of the Catholic faith which are less offensive than certain others. It is indeed a lack of charity needlessly to offend the sensitivities of others in proposing certain Catholic positions. Personal attacks, mockery of dissident faiths, and jaundiced views of non-Catholics are simply inexcusable from the point of view of Christian charity. There is a legitimate and healthy form of discussion which leads to mutual understanding; this does not imply that agreement is reached, but discussions carried on in this way are extremely useful in that they lead the disputants — Protestant, Catholic, Jew, agnostic, or whatever — to a knowledgeable understanding of what others really believe. In this way the images of others which are founded on half-truths are dissipated. This type of understanding is fortunately on the increase in America.[49] Many Catholics are in for a great surprise if they think that Protestants interpret Scripture as they see fit, or that they have no objective norm for doctrine, or that they believe only what they want to believe, or that they practice birth control because it is "the easy way out," or that justification and faith mean that the Protestant is free from all laws so as to act as he might please. Since these caricatures are fairly common among Catholics, a knowledgeable and charitable redress is absolutely necessary if we are to "do truth in charity." The same type of shock is in store for the Protestant who thinks that the Church is one big monolithic organization, whose members have all their thinking done for them by the hierarchy, or that Catholics want

---

[49] See the frank work by R. M. Brown and G. Weigel, *An American Dialogue* (Garden City, N. Y., 1960).

to take over the country and eliminate religious liberty as soon as they become a majority, or that they want to see all laws on divorce eliminated and antibirth-control laws established in every state and public schools abolished. These caricatures ill befit Christian charity and the cause of civil peace. The words of J. C. Murray are very telling in this regard:

> . . . Catholic and Protestant distrust each other's political intentions. There is the memory of the historical clashes in the temporal order; the Irishman does not forget Cromwell any more readily than the Calvinist forgets Louis XIV. Neither Protestant nor Catholic is yet satisfied that the two of them can exist freely and peacefully in the same kind of city. The Catholic regards Protestantism not only as a heresy in the order of religion but also as a corrosive solvent in the order of civilization, whose intentions lead to chaos. The Protestant regards Catholicism not only as idolatry in the order of religion but as an instrument of tyranny in the order of civilization, whose intentions lead to clericalism. Thus, an *odium civile* accrues to the *odium theologicum*.[50]

To distinguish and understand both civil society and Church is essential to any clear conception of the notion of positive tolerance in our pluralistic society. This is why this type of tolerance can only be gained through effort, humility, and true Christian charity.

What is it that we must tolerate? We, as Catholics, cannot tolerate or approve the fact that the other, not of our faith, is in error. I cannot say that the belief expressed in dissident faiths is objectively good, because this is simply not true. I must reprove and never approve that the one who is not of my faith is not living the full revelation of God as God wills it. Error is simply an evil and can never receive either explicit or implicit approval by me as a Catholic. Fidelity to the truth demands this. If I am indifferent toward the truth, I cannot say that I really love the truth. In this respect, the notion of tolerance commonly accepted today, namely an indifference to truth, is a regression, not a progression. Neither — in this conception of indifference — can I say that I truly love the other, for true

---

[50] J. C. Murray, *We Hold These Truths* (New York, 1960), p. 20.

love, by definition, is to will the good of the other. This necessarily implies that I want him to accept the objective truth which God has revealed.

Nevertheless, in order to love my neighbor in a truly Christ-like way, I must respect his subjectivity and his freedom of conscience. Although I reject the errors contained in the religious teachings he holds, I accept him for what he is, and in so accepting him I resolve to revere his conscience. My love must therefore accept and respect the liberty of his faith. The other, thinking that he too has the objective truth, will try to convert me to his own light. I must tolerate this by respecting the honesty and the sincerity of his desire. The more we come truly to love each other, the more pronounced will be the antithesis which separates us. Tolerance is therefore required in order that our love will be strong enough to support that antithesis. Once this love is no longer present, we must both inevitably fall into a vain attempt to "beat" the other in dispute. Our goal will no longer be to convince one another spiritually but to make our own opinions triumph. It is said that the great writer of the early Church, Tertullian, silenced his enemies by his arguments but never won them over to the true faith. Once true love and consideration are lacking in our discussions, there can only be room for intolerance. There are limits for one who tries to convince the other of the truth of his faith. To approach a dialogue on religious belief in any other way than by appeal to reason and rational persuasion is to do violence to the person of the other. The convictions of others impose a limit beyond which I may not force myself. When truth is pushed to violence, the credibility of the faith as a pure spiritual gift is lost; when there is love without truth, then we have infidelity. This love of the person whose conscience I must respect requires some exacting demands if I wish to keep that love from infidelity.

The first requirement of love worthy of the name is a true interior disposition which, in a disinterested way, respects in others the dignity of their human personality. Yet it is impossible for us to penetrate the interiority of others, just as our own interiority is inaccessible to others as such. We must manifest this interior respect of the person *taken concretely as he is*. We have need of various objective elements of signs and symbols in which we incarnate this respect of the human person. In respect of his conscience, no exterior force of any kind may be used to make him act against his formed conscience. Such a polemic, invective or force, would destroy love at its source: the failure to respect the human personality in what is essential to it, the conscience of the other.

A second element of true love is a will to promote the good of the other. We pray that the other comes to see the objective truth as God has revealed it. But given the fact that the other has formed his conscience in a sincere way, I can never promote his good by attempting to force him into an attitude which his conscience could never accept.

Third, love must be reciprocal. It pertains to the essence of love to esteem in each man his dignity and value as a human person, and it would be an error not to wish the same attitude of respect and value for oneself. If it is one-sided, true love cannot reign in the community.

This whole analysis is based on the dignity of the human person and his right to form his own conscience in a sincere and honest way. The subject of these rights is the person himself, because he is independent, irreplaceable, and inviolable in the realization of his moral destiny. If it is true that we must achieve our moral destiny by ourselves, and that we are irreplaceable because of the originality of our activity, then we may also claim as our own everything pertaining to the fulfillment of that destiny. In our personal being lies the source of all our rights; we ourselves are the subjects or bearers of those rights.[51] We can therefore speak of the subjective right to follow our conscience as it has been formed. If a man has such a right

---

[51] John C. Bennett, *Christians and the State* (New York, 1958), pp. 24–50.

in virtue of his personality, others have the absolute obligation to respect that right.[52]

Thus, insofar as man is a spiritual interiority, the person is independent. He can act consciously and freely, which makes him a subject in the strict sense of the word, a being which determines itself. He has to be treated as a person. Whoever encroaches upon the interiority in such a manner that a man can no longer determine his actions consciously and freely degrades this man to an object, violates in him what he is by nature. By virtue of this nature, the person is called to take himself consciously and freely into his own hands as a subject: he has, therefore, an inalienable right to his spiritual integrity. No true love can exist when this integrity is violated.[53]

As a spiritual interiority the person is also irreplaceable. Since his spiritual acts transpire within him, he can only reach his moral destiny by his own actions. To force anyone's conscience either directly or indirectly is to destroy his moral destiny. Man has a personal right to free activity or to personal initiative.[54] But to engage himself, the person must be brought to the point where he becomes capable of taking himself into his own hands and of making his original talents fruitful in his own activities. To violate his right to do this is to violate the moral destiny of the human person.[55]

Man is also inviolable. As a thinking being he is capable of grasping the objective meaning of his personal being, and thus of bringing that meaning into every concrete situation by the judgment of his conscience. Only the objective meaning of our being[56] can effectively lead and direct our actions insofar as they are grasped by our conscience. We must therefore form and follow our conscience. And if that is our duty, all others have the duty of respecting that right which is inherent to our human nature. Once this conscience has been formed according to

---

[52] *Ibid.*, p. 288; also C. Boyer, "Truth and Tolerance," *Unitas*, 14 (1962), 3–16.

[53] *Religion and Freedom* (New York, 1958), p. 33.

[54] J. Maritain, *Man and the State* (Chicago, 1960), pp. 76–107.

[55] *Ibid.*, p. 82. [56] *Ibid.*, p. 90.

prudent judgment, we must follow it at all costs. The fact that a man's conscience can be in error despite his best efforts does not nullify his duty of following it once it is formed.[57] The norm of morality which we must apply to our actions can only reach our actions, then, by way of our judgment of conscience; and since this judgment is based on conscience as subjectively formed, error is always possible. But, since action is necessary to reach our moral destiny, we must follow our conscience.

We have dwelt at some length on the notion of person and personal rights because this is essential to any conception of true Christian love. God is the Author of our natures as well as of revealed truth. Thus He wills that we respect human nature as He has created it and, as a result, that we do no violence to that nature in attempting to lead others to revealed truth. True love demands that I respect this objective order of being. To encroach on any of these requirements of respect for the sacred personality to others is to make the word "love" empty of any meaning.

Yet real love attempts to go as far as it can in willing the good of the other and seeks to do what it can in a positive fashion to bring the other to faith. As we have said, this can only be brought about in love, which implies an absolute respect for the convictions and the conscience of others. This positive attitude implies various elements which we would like to expose now.

1. One of the first and more important elements of positive tolerance as we have described it is that we must accept the good faith of others. This might seem self-evident, but it appears that all too often we refuse to take seriously the claims of others.[58] St. Thomas said that it was the mark of a true Catholic that he take the other person in the best possible sense. As long as the Protestant thinks that all this talk about

---

[57] J. Maritain, *The Rights of Man* (London, 1958), pp. 29–30.
[58] R. M. Brown, "Rules for the Dialogue," *Commonweal*, 71 (1960), 563–566.

"tolerance" in a pluralistic society is simply a subterfuge until such time as the Catholic is in power, no proper attitude of real tolerance can ever exist. Both sides must presuppose that the other is speaking and acting in good faith. If this presupposition is not present, no dialogue and understanding is possible. The accent must be on the second word in the commonly used phrase: "separated brothers."

Men of different beliefs spontaneously wish to triumph over the other, not for the sake of truth, but for the sake of self-affirmation which is pride. At this point, however, the Protestant is more uneasy than the Catholic. The Catholic — because of the tradition of distinction in Catholic theology — can readily distinguish between objective truth and error and its subjective conviction in the mind of the believer. Catholics must continuously emphasize this point lest it be misunderstood by non-Catholics. In tolerance as the Catholic sees it, it is only the objective truth or error which is put into question or rejected, never the person who holds that error as a basic truth.

This basic good will on both sides implies a whole series of attitudes. Positive tolerance will demand that we allow others to contradict us in good faith, without imputing to them impure motives, personal invective or "backbiting" of any kind. This obviously does not mean that we are to sit back and say nothing even against those who attack us in good faith. It simply means that we must never presuppose that such attacks are made in bad faith. It further means that our own response must be on a high and knowledgeable level. We have absolutely no right to doubt, in general and as a basic principle, the good faith of others. Wounding words are totally out of place. Let us simply take one case in point. Many times Catholics use the canonical term "heretic" when referring to separated Christians. In Canon Law the real definition of heretic is one who consciously and willfully remains in a state of contradiction to some revealed dogma of faith.[59] We could never presume to

---

[59] Canon 1325, par. 2, uses the word *pertinaciter*, which means a willful adherence to false doctrine. Implied in this is the element of bad faith.

say that this is true of Protestants. We must clearly distinguish between a material heretic and a formal heretic who knowingly and willfully adheres to false doctrine. Since Protestantism has helped shape the past 400 years of human society, it would be most unjust and false for a Catholic to say that the vast majority of Protestants were formal heretics. The word "heretic" ought to be avoided, because it is a false reference to present-day Protestants. This is not to say that a man could never reject the evident truth if he saw it; this distinct possibility exists. Nevertheless, the judgment that this possibility is fulfilled is a task better left to God than to fallible men.

All this implies a double function if one wishes to arrive at a proper understanding of tolerance. It implies first of all that both parties have a clear understanding of their own faith. Without this understanding there is always the danger that what is of truth (de fide) and what is simply of human tradition and institution will become confused. Such confusion will do more evil than good, for it frustrates any kind of mutual understanding and cooperation on those truths which are held in common and which can serve as norms for carrying on discussions.[60] It also implies that those engaged in any discussion with those not of their faith should have a clear understanding of the faith of the other. Some deep misunderstandings on both sides must be cleared up before we can presume to speak with any kind of authority with a person not of our faith.

If these two conditions are fulfilled, unity will evidently not come about *ipso facto*. This depends on the will of God, and we must wait until He sees fit to clear the difficulties in a more profound perspective; yet these conditions will remove irrational fears and misunderstandings which promote needless strains and difficulties in a pluralistic society. True positive tolerance can gain immensely from such understandings.

2. Another condition is that we learn to see the good which remains in both Christian and non-Christian faiths. Fr. Danielou

---

60 Cf. H. Küng, *The Council, Reform and Reunion* (New York, 1961), pp. 100–128.

has written a rather remarkable book in which he shows how other religions inclusive of Judaism had natural preparations for the fullness of truth given in Christ. "All that is good in these religions comes from God, in respect to whatever intuition they can have of Him through the signs that He gives to them."[61] All too often we tend to emphasize what divides us and fail to note the ties that unite us. True, fidelity to truth demands that we do not minimize our differences,[62] but this does not negate the fact that we do hold certain truths in common. Fr. Congar has emphasized this point in one of his outstanding books.[63] We must attempt to see clearly where we can cooperate for common spiritual and moral endeavors in our increasingly secularistic and pagan Western society. As Pius XI used to say, the various Christian sects have gold in the impure rock of error. To neglect to see this only makes the idea of true positive tolerance even more difficult in our pluralistic society. Centuries have tended to petrify our differences to the point where we are emotionally and psychologically incapable of understanding this element. This was and continues to be the case with the dissident Oriental Churches of the East.[64] What are some of these basic truths we have in common and upon which we can build a positive respect?

If we understand the following correctly, we can even see that the Church has something to gain *accidentally* from a true reintegration of various dissident groups. The true Church may be compared to a tree which has been badly damaged by a storm. Certain large and important branches have been broken off from the trunk even though the tree is essentially the same, living tree. The tree, however, has been weakened. If the fundamental and intimate nature of the Church has not been affected by heresies and schisms, the fact still remains that the

---

61 *The Salvation of Nations* (New York, 1950), p. 23.
62 R. M. Brown, art. cit., p. 565.
63 *Divided Christendom* (London, 1938), pp. 111–160.
64 Y. Congar, *After Nine Hundred Years* (New York, 1960). The whole thesis of the work is to show that the differences between East and West are just as much psychological and emotional as they are doctrinal.

branches that were so lost have been a true misfortune for the Church. She will find a true enrichment in the return of these various bodies to her bosom. Evidently it is not a question of the Church's lacking at any time anything essential which was originally willed and given her by Christ Himself. Neither can we say — in all truth — that anything essential to her constitution could be brought to her by any dissident sect, each constituting, as it were, a fragment of the one true Church which does not as yet exist. Christ has not been unfaithful to His promises to be with His Church until the end of time. She is and always will remain the one, holy, catholic, and apostolic Church. This admitted, we can surely see a great value in the return of dissident groups to the Church and the spiritual and intellectual enrichment of dogma and the virtues. The Protestants' great love of Sacred Scripture as the word of God would be a welcomed trait in a Catholicism which has, perhaps, too long neglected this primary source of divine revelation in its reaction to certain Protestant exaggerations. The cooperation of Catholic and non-Catholic biblical scholars is something that is commonly accepted. It is a well-known fact that Protestant scholarship in the nineteenth and early twentieth centuries has influenced to a large degree our own Catholic biblical revival of the past 50 years.[65] Many practices in the Catholic tradition are beginning to find their way into various Protestant communities which had lost them in their vehement rejection of anything "Roman": such things as community life in monasticism,[66] confession,[67] celibacy,[68] the Eucharist as a true sacrifice,[69] etc. Would not the Lutheran give to the Catholic a profound sense of the gratuity of divine grace, the Calvinist a more intimate sense of the word of God, an Anglican his

[65] For proof of this, one has only to read the first 100 pages of the magnificent book of Jean Levie, *The Bible: Word of God in Words of Men* (New York, 1961).

[66] J. D. Benoit, *Liturgical Renewal* (London, 1955).

[67] M. Thurian, *Confession* (London, 1956).

[68] M. Thurian, *Marriage and Celibacy* (London, 1959).

[69] A. J. B. Higgins, *The Lord's Supper in the New Testament* (London, 1960).

taste for a true and sober liturgical worship? And what shall
we say of the great riches of the element of divine mystery in
the Church and the sacraments which the Orthodox Christians
have retained through the centuries? This is a delicate problem,
and we run the danger here of confusing what is intensive with
what is extensive. The Lutheran, for instance, can never bring
us a part of the essential doctrine on divine grace and adoption
which the Church did not have before. This we cannot admit
for the simple reason that it would not be true. Still, Catholics
can learn much from their separated brothers by observing the
intensity with which they live the truths which they have kept.
It is quite possible that the immediate surroundings of a Catholic do not give this example. Let us simply say that the return
of non-Catholics to the one true fold would draw our attention
to certain spiritual treasures in the Church which we have not
utilized enough. In each case, however, there remains a definite
lived truth in these dissident communities which we have no
right to despise or belittle, in spite of the fact that they are
embedded in a rock of error.

Another case in point is the recent controversy between
Catholics and Protestants on the subject of sanctifying or
created grace. To go into any long history of this question would
be superfluous. The whole story and its evolution is a tragedy
in the time between the great Scholastic period to the revolt
of the sixteenth century.[70] Throughout this nominalistic period,
the true Catholic notion of created or sanctifying grace was distorted by such authors as Ockham and Biel. It was in this
deteriorated state that the reformers rejected the notion of
sanctifying grace. Thus Luther rejected this distorted notion —
thinking it was the official Catholic teaching — and strongly
insisted on the free acceptance by God in place of the notion

[70] L. Bouyer, The Spirit and the Forms of Protestantism (London, 1956),
pp. 70–85; F. Loofs, Leitfaden zur Dogmengeschichte, II (Berlin, 1954), pp.
696–734; M. Lackmann, Zur reformatorischen Rechtfertigungslehre (Stuttgart,
1953), pp. 20–45, etc.

of created grace. It was also under this false notion of the Catholic doctrine on grace that he thought that if one posits the notion of habitual grace, one cannot have a direct union with Christ, except by means of a thing "adhering" to the soul. Following Biel, therefore, Luther will posit an extrinsic justification of the soul with no internal, ontological change in man — for it is evident that if there is not created grace, justification must be extrinsic to man. The means to this is not by any merit of man either before or after, but by simple fiducial and filial faith in the merits and the redemption of Christ. Thus man while still totally corrupt by original sin, still a sinner, begins an ethical renovation by means of this extrinsic justification. The true internal renovation will come only with death. This type of justice must of necessity be the same in all men, and there can be no room for any increase or decrease. The only sin which can destroy this work is the sin against faith. The sanctification of which Luther speaks can produce no merit whatever.

The position of Luther which we have just outlined in simple fashion should be very clear from the background of nominalism of the time. It is well known, for instance, that Luther approved of the teaching of Peter Lombard who identified charity and uncreated grace. Luther clearly recognized the gift of uncreated grace. He rejected created grace, however, because he wanted to express a personal contact with Christ, and not a contact with a "thing." The really unfortunate thing is that because of the dominant nominalistic thinking of the sixteenth century — among both Catholics and reformers — Luther could not understand the meaning of created grace as developed in the true Catholic tradition. The gift of grace as conceived by Biel or Ockham could only be something separate from God, shut off inside the closed system of humanity, with God removed to an arbitrary and inaccessible transcendence. Because nominalism could conceive of no real contact between the creature and the Creator, it presented created grace as an intermediate being, a separate entity in itself, possessed by man apart from the influence of grace.

With the intention of combating Pelagianism, Luther denied any created grace which — as we have already seen — was first proposed by the medieval theologians to combat any such theory. The tragedy of the Reformation is that it did not know the teachings of the great Scholastics but only that of their decadent followers. "In an adequate presentation, such as that of St. Bonaventure, Luther would not have rejected the notion of created grace."[71] So much for a specific example.

It is along these lines that the movement of Ecumenicism has begun in our day.[72] Ecumenicism is a new word, and for each new word there corresponds a new reality which has come into being, e.g., the proletariat of the nineteenth century represented a new working-class population greatly active in the city. A new reality springs up to which a new name is given. The word "ecumenical" has existed for a long time, e.g., the Ecumenical Councils of the Church. But the substantive ecumenicism is a modern word which had its origin about the year 1920. What is the new reality which it designates? It is a new method of trying to establish a visible unity among all Christians by viewing the problem in its entirety. Before, there were partial debates on such things as Calvinism, the Eucharist, etc. Now, it is no longer a question of just one section of truth or doctrine or dissent, but of the problem of divided Christianity as a whole.

Before this new theory with regard to Christian unity, the general attitude was one of opposition, of one argument for another. Discussions between Catholics and Protestants consisted essentially in attacks and counterattacks. We must now revise our ideas. How? Among all the dissident Christians outside of the Roman Communion, there exists today (for the first time in history) what we would call a *Votum Ecclesiae* or a *Votum Catholicitatis*. That is, there are many bodies who

---

[71] Cf. C. Moeller and G. Philips, *The Theology of Grace* (London, 1961), p. 21.   [72] Congar, *After Nine Hundred Years*, pp. 9–36.

believe that they are incomplete, imperfect; they feel that they have something to do with each other; they have a desire for unity in that one true visible Church of Christ. Two considerations are in order here:

a) *Philosophically:* One of the great contributions of modern philosophy has been a better understanding of the twofold character of each particular spiritual act. One aspect aims at a particularity, and the other tends to a universality. When I express something, for example, I must of necessity use modes of expression which are of their very nature limited, imperfect, and particular, e.g., a certain language spoken to a certain people in a certain time in history. But on the other hand, my act which is spiritual has an innate tendency to communicate itself to others, to the spirits of all men. This is what Scholastics called a *desire of the absolute* — a universal truth which, by its nature, reaches all men: this universality is a basic condition whereby one man can enter into communion with all men in a *dialogue.* This type of universality is a sort of "praeecumenism." Hence, men want to go out of their particularities to the universal. Maintaining a confessional faith they also want a universal faith. This tendency is a paradox, but a true tendency today. They want to avoid the "argument-for-argument" style of former days and enter into a true understanding of other sects. These non-Catholics want to expand their ideas into a communion with all other faiths, and finally to come to that one, true, universal truth of Christ and the Church.

b) *Theologically:* Heresy is not only an error (material element). It is also a *pertinacia* (formal element). If then, these Christian bodies are animated by such a universal spirit, can we not exonerate them from the formal element of heresy? This should move us to avoid insults, ridicule, calumnies, etc., and to try to enter with them into a true spirit of communion and understanding. This is dead before it starts if it eliminates apriori any particular group as a group. Our duty is to recognize and respect their positive values for what they are. The Constitution of Rome, *Ecclesia Catholica*, speaks with great respect of non-Catholic values, especially those found in separated Christians.

Confronting such a world and such values, our point of view must change. "Hold on to the good" (1 Thes 5:21). In the past the missions spoke of an "adaptation" of the eternal truth to a certain milieu. Today we have even more, for those to whom we go have positive values to be recognized. The great task of Catholics is to take time out to understand fully separated Christians and to rethink their problems. It takes humility on both sides; and it takes a long time to grow by a slow maturation into this spirit. But it can be a valuable preparation for eventual Christian unity.

3. Another important element in our idea of positive tolerance is that we must take our differences into consideration. To pretend that these differences do not exist would be a false irenicism and indifference. Yet, in taking these differences into consideration, we must do so in charity. To illustrate practically, we may take the example of a Christian who would not knowingly serve pork if he knew that some Jews were to be present at a particular meal. This is simply to show that in all areas of public life we must never expect, much less demand, that a man do anything that would be against his conscience. A concern in this area requires great consideration on all sides, a true study of what can be compatible with the other's conscience in the realm of the public good and a real effort at cooperation in it. We are obliged to collaborate with men of diverse faiths in the building of the city of man, but there are limits beyond which we may not go and beyond which we can never ask another to go. The general rule has been that we observe the other's conscience in the political forum. But there are some stormy problems to be solved here. For example, how far can the state go in respecting the rights of Jehovah Witnesses to refuse blood transfusions for their children? Or what shall we say of the conscientious objector who refuses military service? Even here, the supreme rule of the State must be to respect consciences insofar as this does not endanger the

common good. Given the fact that the two above-mentioned groups are not numerically large enough to pose a grave danger to the public good, the State cannot, it would seem, force the parents to give blood to their child or the conscientious objector to take up arms. This notion, however, of public order is extremely vague, especially in a pluralistic society such as the one in which we live where there is no agreement on common values. The common good seems to be what the heads of government assume it to be. Thus liberty is limited in what is considered to be unhealthy. This is what is commonly called the element of integration — i.e., men cannot live together in any peaceful way unless they are in agreement on certain basic opinions of value, life, and attitudes. When there is perfect integration on one point in society, no one will question it any longer. In such a way, our Western countries under the influence of Christianity have all established monogamic marriage, branding all forms of bigamy as a crime. No one dreams of doing it in any other way. That is why Mormonism is not permitted full religious expression in this regard. Monogamy is integrated into our societies. Because of similar reasons the Jehovah Witnesses have not full freedom in our society. They refuse blood transfusions to their children. It is not that they do not love their children, but their conscience has a different conception of Divine Providence than that of most people in our country. Little liberty is left to them because the idea of medicine has become integrated into our society. True problems are posed when a specific society is not integrated on various points. That is why religious liberty is not very well respected in Moslem countries. It has not become integrated into the mores of the people. Religious freedom is making headway there now because international opinion is being exerted. The same is true in regard to discrimination in the United States. The vast majority of the people agree on the need for integration, but some do not; here is an example of public opinion which is not unanimous, and the result is dissension in the community.

This discussion leads us to the extremely difficult question of the basic foundation of the common good, the natural law and other various problems. In any case, what is certain is that we simply cannot ask another to act against his conscience nor can we cooperate in any action which is against conscience. This poses some extremely agonizing problems in the field of politics and foreign policy. To what degree can a Christian cooperate in a foreign policy which has total nuclear war and indiscriminate retaliation as its ultimate deterrent? This question has divided both the Catholic and Protestant communities in the United States and it probably will continue to do so. What is sure is that a Catholic under pain of sin must have a clear conscience before he acts.[73]

In the area of public policy, some very difficult cases arise for the Catholic in such realms as legislation on education, birth control, and divorce.[74] Fortunately, Catholic theology has developed a whole moral thesis on the relationship between morality and positive laws as such. The lawmaker is not obliged to forbid all evil, especially when he sees that in forbidding some moral evil in an explicit way, a greater evil will ensue. The law is certainly a teacher, but it cannot be so far ahead of the people for whom it is legislated that they find it intolerable law.[75] The law will depend on the *mores* of a specific group of men and not simply on the ideal standard as God wills it. The legislator must balance the ideal of law as the moral teacher of ideals and the actual moral level at which the citizen is. This is what St. Thomas called the *virtus architechtonica* or *prudentia*.[76] The failure on the part of some Catholics to make

---

[73] For a discussion of this aspect in regard to sin in politics, see M. Pribilla, "An den Grenzen der Staatsgewat," *Stimmen der Zeit*, 42 (1947–1948), 420–430.

[74] L. Petrazycki, *Law and Morality* (Cambridge, 1955), p. 60.

[75] E. Barker, "St. Augustine's Theory of Society," *Essays on Government* (Oxford, 1952), pp. 20–26.

[76] See the many texts of St. Thomas, *Summa Theologiae*, I–II, q. 16, a. 2. and 3; q. 90, a. 4; 96, a. 1: "Nevertheless human law does not prescribe concerning all the acts of every virtue: but only in regard to those that are ordainable to the common good — either immediately, as when certain things are done

these elementary distinctions has created much tension in our pluralistic society. Such tension has been created in the argument over the laws on birth control in the New England states.[77] In some cases, it seemed that the Catholic community thought it was being personally attacked. In reality, this was a perfect example of the application of juridical prudence and not directly a theological debate. Many non-Catholics hold in conscience that it is not only licit but, at times, morally obligatory to use artificial means to control conception. We must presuppose that the consciences of these people have been formed in good faith. Given this fact, can the law forbid the public sale of *all* forms of devices for contraception? It would seem that juridical prudence would dictate that such anti-contraceptive laws be repealed. But by the same token, Protestants must recognize the case of conscience of the Roman Catholic population. To disregard this would be to take the same position which has been urged against Catholics who support such legislation: narrow intolerance. It seems that some kind of solution could be found to satisfy the conscience of all concerned. Doctors might legally be permitted to give such information to those who seek it as well as to distribute contraceptives to those who requested them. The prohibition of public sale to minors and of slot machines for distribution could help prevent abuses. Public clinics might also be impowered to sell contraceptives without prosecution when so requested by any citizen. Doctors who objected to the practice could also be protected by law not to give such information. The real trouble starts when either faction forgets the sensitive conscience of the other in this area. Certain types of planned-parenthood evangelicals proselytizing the public for "illumination" make Catholics react with emotion rather than with

---

directly for the common good — or mediately, as when a lawgiver prescribes certain things pertaining to good order, whereby the citizens are directed in the upholding of the common good of justice and peace." *Ibid.*, I–II, q. 16, a. 2.

[77] For a full report on this legislation, see the work of a Catholic, Norman St. John-Stevas, *Birth Control and Public Policy* (Santa Barbara, Calif., 1960); also his *Life, Death, and the Law* (Bloomington, Ind., 1961).

reason. Another easing of tension would be to leave the distribution of this type of information to private groups and not to inject the issue into government expenditures. This last attempt will only cause ill will and emotionalism; in the long run, it will meet with failure because the community as a whole is not at all agreed on its morality, let alone its legislative enforcement or aid. True positive tolerance demands a conservation of both consciences and an equitable solution to this vexing problem. For the Catholic or the Protestant or the Jew not to take into consideration the conscience of the other is a flagrant violation of any true tolerance which is practiced in charity.

4. We must also and above all pray for each other. Our very Christian engagement commands us to pray for our enemies; how much more must we pray for those, who, in a very true sense, are our brothers in Christ, who have been consecrated by the waters of baptism and faith in Christ the Savior. Any other attitude on the part of either Catholic or Protestant (or Jew, insofar as we have the same common Father of the Old Testament) is a mockery and a blight on the sacred name of Christian. As a Catholic, I must pray for the temporal and eternal good of the other in an absolutely real and true sense. I pray that my Protestant brother will someday come to the fullness of God's truth in the Church, but I know that this is a gift of God; in the meanwhile, I must pray that God, in His mysterious ways, will lead the other to Himself. I must humbly leave this prayer to the Father of light, who alone can enlighten and lead the will without forcing it in any way by His grace. We pray that all men receive the fullness of truth, but if they do not seem to do so, the answer must be left to God in mystery. Thus, in the words of St. Paul: "I urge therefore, first of all, that supplications, prayers, intercessions, and thanksgivings be made for all men. This is good and agreeable in the sight of God, Our Savior, who wishes all men to be saved and to come to the knowledge of the truth."[78] Our ultimate prayer, as Chris-

---

[78] 1 Tm 2:1–3.

tians, must be that tolerance disappear and that unity reign even here on earth. Our prayer must be, without reservation, the prayer of Christ when He said: "that they may be one even as we are one." If this were simply a human prayer on our part, we would indeed be tempted to despair because of our seemingly insurmountable differences. But it is the very prayer of the Son of God, and "no Christian (or Jew for that matter) is entitled to believe only in what is humanly possible, for what is impossible to men is possible for God. What we must confess to each other (Protestant, Catholic, and Jew) in penance and yet in hope, is that we do disagree and that we agree that it is wrong to disagree."[79]

In this spirit there are certain types of prayers and invocations which we can pray together, e.g., the Our Father or some prayer from the books of the Old Testament. But for one of a different communion to participate actively in the communion and services of another would be a betrayal of the truth. This must be a strict rule of conscience, for if I believe that the Eucharist is the real and true body, blood, soul, and divinity of Jesus Christ present by the liturgical action of the priest, I cannot in conscience participate in certain Protestant services which consider the Eucharist a simple memorial brought to mind by drinking grape juice. I respect the conviction of my Protestant brother, even though I consider it false, just as I expect the same reverence from him for my own conviction. To be accused of intolerance in this respect would be, once again, to try to force my conscience to perform an act which I consider false worship. Loyalty to the truth demands this. This does not exclude, of course, a certain "passive" attendance at Protestant services permitted Catholics under certain circumstances. In such a case, it is the respect, e.g., for a dead person or for a particular marriage, which prompts my presence, not the worship itself.

In this regard, there is one point which is a grave source of difficulty for many Protestants and Jews concerning the Catholic

---

[79] R. M. Brown, art. cit., in *Commonweal*, p. 566.

faith. It is a difficulty which indirectly affects them and for which they feel a particular antipathy. It is the question of the Church's attitude toward mixed marriages (a marriage between a Catholic and a non-Catholic). In general, in the Code of Canon Law, the Church forbids such matrimonies for her children,[80] unless there are grave reasons for dispensing from such a prohibition. In such a case, however, the non-Catholic party must agree to let the Catholic free to practice his or her religion and must also agree, in writing, that any children born from such a marriage must be raised as Catholics. This is indeed a stumbling block for many non-Catholics, who quickly accuse the Church of intolerance. Yet, if the question is examined logically, the solution of the Church is very clear and reasonable. It is readily agreed by both Protestants and Catholics that the marriage of Christians must be founded in God in order to succeed. The rapidly mounting divorce rates in the United States are bringing this home to all Christians living in our secularistic society. For a Catholic, moreover, marriage is a sacrament, and the children from that marriage must be raised in the faith since the Catholic cannot permit that those intrusted to him or her by God be brought up in error. This is, for the Catholic, a matter of conscience. He holds by faith that his obligation to rear his children as Catholics is willed by God. Therefore, knowingly to permit his children to be brought up in error would be against his conscience.

Yet what of the Protestant party? Does he not have a conscience also? Should not his rights be respected? First of all, it must be said that the Church forces no one to sign such promises. If the non-Catholic party does so, it is through his own free will. The Church strongly discourages such marriages. She knows that matrimony is an institution involving intimate and complete selflessness, where everything must be shared and given in full. She knows, too, that, when a deeply personal and all-embracing thing as religion cannot be shared, great tension will arise between the married parties. There is not

---

[80] Canon 1060.

that complete giving of self because there is not a complete sharing in so important an element as religion. The Church, knowing that many of these marriages end up badly, therefore discourages them. The non-Catholic party is free. Actually, in the logic of his faith, he should come to the very same conclusion as the Catholic, as Karl Barth has already pointed out.[81] His conclusion is absolutely true and if such a situation were to come about, no marriage between a Catholic and non-Catholic could be possible. Actually this would be the ideal as far as the Church is concerned.

Yet some non-Catholics feel that they can engage themselves under such conditions. The Church does not suspect their motives and if they can, in conscience, submit to these requirements, the Church will respect their will and allow the marriage to take place. In such a case, what is the motive of the non-Catholic? Indifference? Closeness to the Church? This is entirely his concern and the Church does not presume to judge him.

This attitude of the Church will seem intolerant only to him for whom truth means nothing. If both parties were logical in this conception, we would applaud both of their decisions not to marry as the most perfect solution.

It is sometimes also objected that the Catholic is "forced" to such a condition by the Church. Catholics, these critics hold, are not free not to follow what the Church tells them. Such an attitude, common enough among non-Catholics, betrays a total misconception of the position of the Church in the relationship of the Catholic with God. The Protestant conception is that there is a direct relationship between man and God with no intermediaries, neither of Church nor priesthood. The Catholic faith holds, however, that the Church, in matters of faith and morals, speaks to the Catholic with the very voice of God. This is what K. Barth calls "idolatry" and what the Catholic calls the faithful spouse of Christ who teaches him objective truth concerning God in Christ's own name. Yes, it

---

[81] *Dogmatik*, III, 14 (1951 ed.), p. 251.

is absolutely true that the Catholic must always follow his conscience in each of his actions from a subjective point of view. Yet he must strive to form his conscience so that it will conform as much as possible to the objective revelation of God given to him in and through the Church since Christ speaks to him there. The Catholic is infallibly sure by his faith that Christ speaks to him in the Church. It is up to the Catholic to form his conscience according to this objective norm. If the Catholic comes to a conclusion different from that of the Church, then he has a truly erroneous conscience and can no longer really be considered a real Catholic. We have seen various examples of this in the recent dispute over integration in New Orleans. The Church simply proposes to the Catholic what is his duty before God, and the Catholic who recognizes the voice of Christ in her listens to her words. Such is the Catholic faith. One may disagree with it, but one cannot deny the logical force and sincere attitude toward the truth in the position of the Catholic Church in this matter.

It has been suggested, however, in certain responsible Catholic circles that certain ceremonies and procedures be changed in order not to offend the non-Catholic party needlessly. Thus, it has been suggested that once the non-Catholic party has promised to abide by the above condition of mixed marriage, no further "signing" of documents be required. It seems to cast doubt on the word of the one who has promised). This is a legitimate observation and it seems that pastors could be given this power to dispense from the signing of documents according to their discretion. Again, it is observed, why deny so much of the religious ceremonies to couples who are entering a mixed marriage? On the contrary, it would seem that such couples need all the spiritual consolation possible because of the added difficulties and strains in their married life. It does not seem totally out of order to suggest, as many leading Catholic moralists have done, that certain ceremonies of a religious nature be performed at these marriages, possibly a low Mass accompanying the marriage with opportunity for the Catholic party to communicate. Such ceremonies would only serve to strengthen the religious nature of this sacred event instead of a quick and almost unreligious ceremony that is performed now. These practical solutions will vary from country to country and no general rule can be established. It is not, however, disrespectful to suggest that such observations be taken seriously by those in authority.

5. Finally, we must consider the notion of education in the type of positive tolerance of which we have been speaking in these pages. As we have already seen, modern tolerance understood as indifference is no advance but a regression. But with the points we have developed in a positive fashion, i.e., mutual understanding, mutual trust, and mutual cooperation within the confines of conscience, we can make real progress in the notion of tolerance and peace in our pluralistic society. True tolerance makes very high moral demands: it is not simply a cliché of "brotherhood" uttered in various editorials or political speeches. It is the fruit of hard labor and of love. Men are not born with tolerance; men, on the contrary, have a natural penchant to be aggressive and self-affirmative even (and possibly, above all) in religious matters. We have already seen both the demands of truth and of love. Both are personal disciplines due to the dignity of each human being once he has formed his own conscience in good faith. Man possesses this dignity by the very fact that he was created in the image of God,[82] and this is the basic justification for mutual respect. This respect allows us complete sincerity when confronting others to reveal our differences, but also our agreements. This respect and consideration of both similarity and dissimilarity allows us to live together in peace and love. We must never sacrifice truth or charity. There will be tensions in trying to keep a balance between the two, but such tensions can be viewed peacefully by men of good will and solutions for common endeavors can be found.

----

[82] "The image of God in us," says Origen, "may be obscured by our own negligence but it cannot be completely destroyed through our wickedness." *In Genesis*, hom. 13, 4.

In the education of the young, we must emphasize what we have brought out in the discussion of positive tolerance understood as both truth and charity. There is a great danger, especially in parochial schools, of a divisiveness, since affective antipathy can easily be engendered when we are separated in diverse schools. There is danger, yet it is not a danger which is insurmountable. The mere fact of being in the same room in the public school with other people day after day does not necessarily bring unity and tolerance. There are people who have been living together all their lives in apartment buildings who do not even know their next-door neighbor. This danger in our schools is not inevitable. To emphasize the Catholic faith, for instance, by belittling other religions is a very poor approach to this problem of a pluralistic society — if not downright disastrous. We must show the truths of our faith and fully defend them. We must also show the errors of false religious and dissident Christian communities. Yet, we should also stress the positive and truthful elements present in these diverse communities. Even the ancient Fathers of the Church saw that an overpreoccupation with the negative and defensive can lead to unhealthy attitudes. We become negative and defensive ourselves. Our apologetics — which has been, for the most part, nourished on anti-Protestant themes — could use some more positive notes than have been given in the past. In our schools, we must always speak with respect of others not of our faith, avoiding wounding expressions and accusations of bad faith. We must always emphasize that they are in error. The simple truth demands this. But we must also emphasize that in charity we owe them respect for their formed consciences as human beings, that we must pray sincerely for them, that we must cooperate with them in endeavors which concern the public good and not hold back because the initiative or the idea did not come from a "Catholic." Above all, he who teaches must give the example to the children entrusted to him. We teach not only by what we say but also by what we do and many times by what we do *not* do or say.

In this way, there will reign the greatest amount of true peace based on truth and charity which can be allotted to sinful and unfaithful men here below. As Pope John XXIII has said so well: the cause of our divisions is equally divided. Let us forget the wounding and uncharitable past shared by us both and concentrate on the present and the future. Only in such an atmosphere and under such conditions can the freedom of the sons of God flourish and grow.

Bibliographical Note

The following annotated works are intended as general references for those who wish to continue their readings on the notion of tolerance as well as on the notion of Church-State relationships.

1. Aubert, Roger, La Théologie Catholique au milieu du XXe Siècle. Tournai: Casterman, 1954.
2. ———— Le Pontificat de Pie IX. Paris: Bloud et Gay, 1952.
   A general conspectus of theology in the twentieth century covering a range of such subjects as liturgy, Bible, etc. It touches briefly the importance of tolerance in the twentieth century.
   The second historical work covers that difficult period of the Church's history when she had to face the modern world. Many affirmations against liberty by the Popes have a historical setting which cannot be neglected in the history of tolerance.
3. Bennett, John C. Christians and the State. New York: Charles Scribner's Sons, 1958.
   A foremost American Protestant scholar gives his own views on the matter from an American point of view. Bennett is very sympathetic to various Catholic theological bases for religious freedom.
4. Berkouwer, G. C. Recent Developments in Roman Catholic Thought. Grand Rapids, Michigan: Eerdmans, 1958.
   Traces some developments in Catholic theological thought on tolerance. Valuable for various Catholic citations.
5. Brown, Robert M., and Weigel, G. An American Dialogue. Garden City, N. Y.: Doubleday, 1960.
   Both authors give frank opinions of each other and their common fears and hopes. One of the first in the "dialogue" of understanding in Catholic-Protestant relation in America.

6. Cogley, John, and others. *Religion in America*. New York: Meridian Books, 1958.

A book similar in purpose to the preceding, but embracing a wider group, including Jews. The purpose was to expose religious agreements and disagreements in the pluralistic society that is America.

7. Congar, Yves, and others. *Tolerance and the Catholic*. New York: Sheed and Ward, 1954.

One of the first corporate Catholic attempts to justify the notion of tolerance against a historical, biblical, and theological background. Highly recommended.

8. Cullmann, O. *Dieu et César*. Paris: Delachoux el Niestlé, 1956.

Tries to define the relationship between the Church and State on the basis of New Testament theology. A scriptural study of the problem.

9. D'Arcy, Eric. *Conscience and its Right to Freedom*. New York: Sheed and Ward, 1961.

Traces the notion of conscience in the great Scholastics and especially in St. Thomas. Attempts to draw conclusion from Thomas' thought that the erroneous conscience is binding absolutely.

10. De Albornoz, Carrillo A. F., ed. *Roman Catholicism and Religious Liberty*. Geneva: World Council of Churches, 1959.

A complete compilation of texts from various Catholic authors attesting to the notion of religious liberty and tolerance. Very valuable for source material.

11. De Boer, Cecil. *Responsible Protestantism: Essays on the Christian's Role in a Secular Society*. Grand Rapids, Mich.: Eerdmans, 1957.

The responsibility of Protestants to take a Christian attitude in their relationship to the secular and political world.

12. De Lagarde, Georges. *La naissance de l'esprit laique*. Louvain: Editions E. Nauwelaerts, 1956. 5 vols.

A historical study tracing the beginnings of secularism in modern thought from the end of the Middle Ages.

13. De Montcheuil, Yves. *Guide for Social Action*. Chicago: Fides Publishers, 1954.

14. ——— *La conversion du monde*. Bruxelles, 1954.

15. ——— *l'église et le monde actuel*. Paris: Aubier, 1945.

A French Jesuit who attempts to give Christian perspectives to the temporal order and the body politic. Chapters on civil tolerance are interesting in each of these three books.

16. Doerries, Herman. *Constantine and Religious Liberty*. New Haven: Yale University Press, 1960.

Traces the notion of religious liberty and tolerance from the early days of the Church until the time of Constantine.

17. Feltin, Cardinal, and others. *Christianity and Freedom*. London: Hollis and Carter, 1955.

Various essays by Frenchmen on the importance and necessity of tolerance in various fields of human endeavor: theology, literature, politics, etc.

18. Hales, E. E. Y. *The Catholic Church in the Modern World*. Garden City, N. Y.: Hanover House, 1958.

19. ———— *Pio Nono*. New York: P. J. Kenedy, 1954.

A historical conspectus of the difficult period of Church's history when she first began to face the modern period. Also valuable for understanding the milieu with regard to freedom during this period.

20. Hartmann, Albert. *Toleranz und Christliche Glaube*. Frankfurt am Main: Verlag Josef Knecht, 1955.

A general exposé and defense of religious tolerance understood as the respect due the dignity of the human person. Opposes relativism.

21. Jassens, L. *Droits Personnels et Autorité* Louvain: Ed. Nauwelaerts, 1954.

A defense of the foundations on which the rights of man are based. Attempts to show what they imply, including the notion of love and religious liberty.

22. Kerwin, Jerome C. *Catholic Viewpoint on Church and State*. New York: Hanover House, 1960.

A general and popular exposé of the relationship between Church and State. General principles affecting this relationship with specific application to the situation in the United States.

23. Lecler, Joseph. *l'Eglise et la souveraineté de l'Etat*. Paris, 1946.

24. ———— *Tolerance and the Reform*. New York: Associated Press, 1960. 2 vols.

25. ———— *The Two Sovereignties*. Westminster, Md.: Newman, 1956.

Monumental works tracing the history of tolerance from the beginning of the Church down to and including the Reformation and discussing the relationship between Church and State in modern society.

26. Leclercq, Jacques. *l'Etat ou la politique*. Namur: Wesmael-Charlier, 1958.

The rights of man and of the State are clearly brought out by this social philosopher. Shows the basis on which the human person can claim his rights and his obligations to the State.

27. Locke, John. *The Second Treatise on Civil Government* and a *Letter Concerning Toleration*, ed. by J. W. Gough. Oxford: At the Univerity, 1946.

    One of the first modern documents on this subject. A truly remarkable piece for the times in which Locke lived.

28. Marcel, Gabriel. *Phénomenologie et dialectique de la tolerance.* Paris, 1940.

    Tries to justify the idea of tolerance from an existential analysis of who and what man is. Mostly based on the analysis of love.

29. Maritain, Jacques. *Man and the State.* Chicago: University of Chicago Press, 1951.

30. ———— *Freedom in the Modern World.* New York: Sheed and Ward, 1955.

31. ———— *The Rights of Man.* London: Goeffrey Bles, 1958.

    Maritain's preoccupation is with the rights of man in the face of the State, based on his dignity as a person and a son of God. On this basis, he argues for a complete respect for the conscience of others vis-à-vis the State.

32. Murray, John C., and others. *The Role of the Independent School in American Democracy.* Milwaukee: Marquette University Press, 1956.

    Cited simply as an example of the many works in print defending the existence of the Catholic and private school and the parents' right to send him and a corresponding demand in justice for public support for them lest this right become a mockery.

33. O'Brien Hanley, Thomas. *Their Rights and Liberties.* Westminster. Md.: Newman Press, 1959.

    A history of tolerance and religious freedom in the first American Catholic colony of Maryland and its relationship with the rest of the American colonies.

34. O'Brien, William F. *Justice Reed and the First Amendment.* Washington, D. C.: Georgetown University Press, 1958.

    An expert in constitutional law examines the influence of Reed on the interpretation of the freedom of religious clause of the American Constitution.

35. O'Connell, David A. *Christian Liberty.* Westminster: Newman Press, 1952.

    Attempts to show in what Christian liberty principally consists, namely, spiritual freedom from which flow all other liberties.

36. Pierce, C. A. *Conscience in the New Testament.* London: SCM Press, 1958.

    A scriptural commentary of the meaning of conscience and its formation in the texts of the New Testament. Very important as a source book for a background of religious freedom and tolerance.

37. Powers, Francis J. *Religious Liberty and the Police Power of the State*. Washington, D. C.: 1948.

The author attempts to show the definite limitation of the state in regard to religious liberty. He concludes from various theological and philosophical arguments to full toleration.

38. Rommen, Heinrich A. *The State in Catholic Thought*. St. Louis: B. Herder Book Co., 1955.

Traces the notion of the State in Catholic theory and practice. One of the finest syntheses on the subject in the English language.

39. St. John-Stevas, Norman. *Birth Control and the Public Policy*. Fund for the Republic, 1960.

40. ——— *Obscenity and the Law*. Bloomington, Ind.: Indiana University Press, 1960.

41. ——— *Life, Death and the Law*. Bloomington, Ind.: Indiana University Press, 1961.

Attempts to show from a juridical point of view that the Catholic attitude toward legislation cannot be simply a moral one, but must take into consideration the concrete situation and moral level of the people for whom the law is intended.

42. Tussman, Joseph, ed. *The Supreme Court on Church and State*. New York: Oxford University Press, 1962.

A straight listing of texts of all Supreme Court references of cases involving Church and State. Valuable for reference work on Church and State.

43. Vermeersch, Arthur. *Tolerance*. New York: Benziger Bros., 1912.

One of the first Catholic works to pose the problem as theological. He came to the conclusion that tolerance is a basic and theological necessity in any pluralistic society.

44. Weigel, G. *Faith and Understanding in America*. New York: Macmillan, 1959.

Attempts to understand various Protestant lines of thought current in modern America to illuminate citizens on this subject.

45. Weigel, G., and others. *American Catholics: A Protestant-Jewish View*. New York: Sheed and Ward, 1960.

A frank statement of expectations and fears concerning certain Catholic teachings and attitudes in America today from both Protestant and Jewish sources. Valuable for understanding non-Catholic fears about American Catholicism.

46. Wood, H. G. *Religious Liberty Today*. Cambridge: At the University, 1944.

A general perspective on the progress which religious liberty has made in the world in general today, its foundation and future hopes.

47. Woodruff, D. *Church and State*. New York: Hawthorn Books, 1961.

A popular exposé intended for the average layman, which explains some basic notions on the relations between Church and State and the duties and obligations binding each.

48. *Standard Texts in Latin, and Special Works*. Capello, P. *Summa Juris Publici Ecclesiastici*. Rome, 1928.

Standard text which exposes same doctrine as No. 47 with regard to Church and State.

49. Lo Grasso, John. *Ecclesia et Status*. Rome: Gregorian University Press, 1952.

Includes most of the most important texts of the Popes through the ages. Extremely valuable as reference.

50. Ottaviani, Cardinal. *Compendium Juris Publici Ecclesiastici*. Ed. 4. emendata. Citta del Vaticano: Typis Polyglottis Vaticanis, 1954.

Gives the ordinary exposé of the relation between Church and State, especially in the second volume. His theory, as is well known, is "thesis-hypothesis," understood as union of Church and State where this is possible — and this as an ideal.

51. Struzo, Luigi. *Church and State*. Notre Dame, Ind.: University of Notre Dame Press, 1962. 2 vols.

Monumental historical exposé of the relations which have governed these two societies through the centuries. Recently put into paperback.

52. Miscellanea. De la Briere, Yves, and others. *Miscellanea Veermeersch*. Rome, 1955.

A general theological exposition and defense of religious tolerance by various Catholic theologians. They argue from a scriptural, dogmatic, philosophical, and practical point of view to the thesis that all in the State must be granted religious toleration and liberty.

ARTICLES AND PAMPHLETS

1. Adeney, W. F. "Toleration," *Dictionary of Religion and Ethics*, V. 12 (1921), pp. 350–375.
2. Alter, Karl J. "Nineteen Questions about a Catholic President," *Catholic Mind*, LXVII (September–October, 1960), pp. 440–449.
3. Barrett, Patricia. "Church and State: A Bibliography — I," *Theol-*

ogy Digest, VII (Autumn, 1959), 185–190.

4. ——— "Church and State: A Bibliography — II," *Theology Digest,* VIII (Winter, 1960), 59–63.

5. Bevenot, M. "Thesis and Hypothesis," *Theological Studies,* XV (1954), 441 ff.

6. Charriere, François. "The Catholic Church and Religious Tolerance," *Catholic Mind,* LVI (July–August, 1958), 293–304.

7. "Church and State — An American Catholic Tradition," *Harper,* CCVII (November, 1953), 63–67.

8. Congar, Yves. "L'Eglise et l'Etat," *Catholicisme,* I (1946), col. 516–525.

9. ——— "Proselytisme et Evangelisatim," *Rythmes du Monde,* 14 (1947), 26–38.

10. Connery, John. "Religious Pluralism and Public Morality," *America,* C. (February 21, 1959), 597–599.

11. Cour, R. F. "Recent Teachings of the Supreme Court on the Subject of Church and State," *Records of the American Catholic Historical Society of Philadelphia,* LXVIII (September, 1957), 96–105.

12. Cushing, Richard Cardinal. "The Christian and the Community," Pastoral Letter, (1960).

13. De Bovis, Andre. "l'Eglise dans la societé temporelle," *Nouvelle Révue Théologique,* LXXIX (March, 1957), 225–247.

14. Ellis, John T. "American Catholicism in 1960: An Historical Perspective," *American Benedictine Review* (March–June, 1960), 3–5.

15. Gerlier, Peter Cardinal. "The Co-existence of Believers and Unbelievers," *Cross Currents* VI (1956), 285–293.

16. Guerrero, E. "Mas sobre la libertad religiosa en España," *Razon y fe,* CSLIX (1954), 331 ff.

17. Journet, Charles. "Droit de la vrai religion et tolerance civile des cultes," *Nova et vetera,* XXVI (1951), 6 ff.

18. Lercaro, Giacomo Cardinal. "Religious Tolerance in Catholic Tradition," *Catholic Mind,* LXIII (January–February, 1960), 12–24.

19. Lecler, Joseph. "A propos de la distinction de la these et de l'hypothese," *Recherches de sciences religeuse,* XLI (1953), 532 ff.

20. ——— "La Papauté moderne et la liberté de conscience," *Etudes,* CCXLIX (1946), 289 ff.

21. ——— "Les formes modernes de l'intolerance," *Etudes,* CCXI (1932), 274 ff.

22. Leclercq, Jacques. "Etat Chrétien et liberté dans l'Eglise," *Vie Intellectuelle* (February, 1949), 99 ff.

23. Lener, Salvatore, "l'ordine dello Stato e l'ordine della Chiesa. I,"

La Civilta Cattolica, CIX (August, 1958), 234–249.

24. ———— "l'ordine dello Stato e l'ordine della Chiesa. II." (August 16, 1958), 350–364.

25. ———— "l'ordine dello Stato e l'ordine della Chiesa. III," (September 6, 1958), 463–478.

26. Michel, A. "Tolerance," *Dictionaire de la théologie Catholique*, V (1927), 1208–1223.

27. Murray, John C. "Contemporary Orientations of Catholic Thought on Church and State in the Light of History," *Theological Studies*, X (June, 1949), 177 ff.

28. ———— "Current Theology on Religious Liberty," *Theological Studies*, X (September, 1949), 409 ff.

29. ———— "Freedom of Religion: I. The Ethical Problem," *Theological Studies*, VI (June, 1945), 229–286.

30. ———— "Governmental Repression of Heresy," The Catholic Theological Society of America, *Proceedings*, 1948.

31. ———— "St. Robert Bellarmine on the Indirect Power," *Theological Studies*, IX (December, 1948), 491–535.

32. ———— "Challenges Confronting the American Catholic," *Catholic Mind*, LVII (May–June, 1959), 196–200.

33. "On Religious Toleration," an American reprint, 1960.

34. Pribilla, Max. "Dogmatische Intoleranz und burgerliche Toleranz," *Stimmen der Zeit*, CXLIV (April, 1949), 28–29.

35. "Protestant-Roman Catholic Dialogue," *Christianity and Crisis*, XIX (June 8, 1959).

36. *Religion and the Free Society*. Santa Barbara, Calif. Fund for the Republic pamphlets, 1958. See also *The Churches and the Public*, 1960, and *Religion and the Schools*, 1959, all in this same series.

37. Rumble, Leslie, "Pitfalls of Pluralism," *The Homiletic and Pastoral Review*, LX (September, 1960), 1121–1140.

38. Rouquette, Robert. "Pie XII et la tolerance," *Etudes*, CCLXXX (1954), 246 ff.

39. Soe, Niels. "The Theological Basis of Religious Liberty," *Ecumenical Review*, XI (October, 1958), 36–42.

40. Schoeningh, Franz J. "What is Christian Politics," *Commonweal*, 53 (November 24, 1950), p. 174.

41. Vialatoux, Joseph, and Latreille, Andre. "Christianisme et laicite," *Esprit*, XLVI (October, 1949), 420 ff.

42. Von Kuhnelt-Leddihn, Erik. "Katholische toleranz," *Wort und Wahrheit*, IV (1949), 355 ff.

43. Weigel, G. *Church-State Relations*. Baltimore, Md.: Helicon Press, 1960.

INDEX

Adenauer, 71

Alexander VIII, condemnation of Jansenism, 141

Ambrose, St., Church and State, 64

Anabaptists, 125, 127

Apologetics, reorientation of, 186

Aufklärung, 132; rationalism, 120, 122; significant value of, 131; and tolerance, 128

Augustine, St., on belief, 150, 151; Christian, citizen of two worlds, 80; Church and State, 64; free will and faith, 155; on grace and merit, 156; integration of temporal and religious spheres, 16

Automation, need for theological interpretation of, 42

Baptism, eschatological aspect of, 80; nature of, 79

Barth, Karl, 12; mixed marriage, 183

Belief, definition of, 146

Bellarmine, St. Robert, polemic character of ecclesiology, 65; theory of indirect subordination, 118

Benoit, P., incarnationalism, 20 f; redemption for all creation, 20–21

Bible, optimistic humanism of, 20

Biblical anthropology, Pauline meaning of, 21

Biel, misunderstanding of created grace, 172

"Body," New Testament meaning of, 8

Bonaventure, St., true understanding of grace, 174

Boniface II, 63

Bossuet, integration of temporal and religious sphere, 16

Bouyer, L., meaning of terrestrial realities, 17

Buber, Martin, "I-Thou" relationship, 158

Cana and Pre-Cana Conferences, 87

Cappello, P., 144

Catholic action, definition of, 81

Catholic Church, see Church

Cerfaux, Msgr., laity and royal priesthood, 72

Chamot, 24

Charles, Pierre, incarnationalism, 21; sense of created things, 23

Chenu, M. D., 26, 30

Christian Family Movement, 85, 87

Christian humanism, definition of, 84

Christians, fundamental vocation of, 62; source of dignity, 62

Church, enrichment through reunion, 170; enrichment through unity, 171; as objective norm for her members, 184; as "sign," 152

Church and State, "duo sunt" formula of Pope Gelasius, 129; objectives of, 117; theory of indirect subordination, 118; "thesis-hypothesis" theory, 118, 119, 121

Civil authority, proper end of, 153

Commonweal, lay journal, 95

Communism, leading to self-destruction, x

Confirmation, given for apostolate of witness, 68; "sacrament of lay apostle," 69

Congar, Yves M.-J., 16, 26; freedom in the Church, 92; "hierarchiology" vs. ecclesiology, 65, 130; meaning of terrestrial realities, 17; status of ecclesiology, 63; truths common to all religions, 170

Conscience, duties of, 166; freedom of, 147; obligation of, 160

Consensus fidelium, and voice of the Spirit, 94

Creation, Catholic conception of, 12; Christ, its originating principle, 10;